Learning the Way

Learning the Way

Reclaiming Wisdom from the Earliest Christian Communities

CASSANDRA D. CARKUFF WILLIAMS

THE
ALBAN
INSTITUTE
Herndon, Virginia
www.alban.org

The Alban Institute
2121 Cooperative Way, Suite 100
Herndon, VA 20171

Unless otherwise noted, all Scripture quotations are from the New Revised Standard Version of the Bible, copyright © 1989, Division of Christian Education of the National Council of the Churches of Christ in the United States of America, and are used by permission.

Scripture quotations marked CEV are from the Contemporary English Version of the Bible, copyright © 1991, 1992, 1995 by the American Bible Society, and are used by permission.

Cover design by Tobias Becker, Bird Box Design.

Library of Congress Cataloging-in-Publication Data

Williams, Cassandra Carkuff.
  Learning the way : reclaiming wisdom from the earliest Christian communities / Cassandra D. Carkuff Williams.
      p. cm.
  Includes bibliographical references.
  ISBN 978-1-56699-385-2
  1. Discipling (Christianity) 2. Discipling (Christianity) —History. 3. Church history—Primitive and early church, ca. 30-600. I. Title.

  BV4520.W49 2008
  253—dc22
                        2008049482

    09   10   11   12   13   VP   5   4   3   2   1

Dedicated to my brother, Doug,
in honor of the comfort we were to each other growing up,
and in hope for the peace that is yet to come.

Contents

Foreword

I was very pleased to learn that this book by Cassandra Williams would be published by the Alban Institute. Alban has consistently provided important books on congregational life for church leaders. But too few have given a specific focus on congregational education, one of the most important functions of any congregation. With this title Alban offers church leaders—pastors, laypersons, and educational program staff—a resource for building a framework for authentic Christian education and discipleship in congregations.

Once, over lunch during a conference, I asked a church historian and cultural critic if he would ever identify a point at which a congregation would cease to be "Christian." His answer was no. Given the perpetual struggle of the church, over the centuries, to avoid cultural captivity with its resulting loss of an authentic voice of hope, I found his response surprising. Williams's book offers a counterargument to the idea that a congregation is church merely because of what it may look like or call itself. Williams unapologetically identifies what is required to be an authentic Christian church: the ongoing presence of Jesus Christ at the center of community. The book offers a reminder of the church's cultural and historical roots, and thereby provides congregational leaders an important perspective for how the shape of its life and mission needs to be.

Conversational in style but appropriately critical, *Learning the Way* is grounded in historical perspective which provides a responsible corrective to faddish notions about Christian education and discipleship. Williams reminds her readers of one of the most important truths for understanding the nature of Christian discipleship: discipleship requires life in community. By that she does not mean a "feeling of community" or a "sense of family" or other notions that reduce community to a feeling or predilection. She correctly identifies the nature of what constitutes community, including the presence and inclusion of children—for true communities are generative. By providing an overview of the first three generations of the Christian faith, Williams provides a clue as to how the Way was formatted both by its cultural and historical context, and also by its nature: Christianity was a movement and corporate way of life before it was an organized religion. Reclaiming the appropriate context of discipleship formation in the life of the community of faith provides a critical corrective to one of the most damaging elements of contemporary Christianity, the overfocus on individualistic understandings of faith and discipleship.

The field of Christian education is experiencing major shifts in its understanding of the nature of educating in faith and the ways and means for achieving it. On some fronts congregational educators are changing the ways they practice teaching and learning through their continuing openness to what the social sciences show about learning organizations, group dynamics, and individual domains like multiple intelligences and brain research applied to pedagogy. At the same time, congregational educators are reclaiming their roots and are favoring terms like formation over education. In my own denomination it is rarer today to find educational program staff with the title Minister of Christian Education. More and more common are titles that are expressions of themes: Pastor of Spiritual Formation, Minister of Spirituality, Associate Pastor of Christian Formation, Minister of Congregational Development, etc. While it is evident that most congregations don't know what those terms may mean, exactly, or what that educational staff person will do aside from keeping traditional church education programs running, there are fresh voices calling for approaches to educating in faith that allow for a move toward formation in community rather than a school for learning, narrowly understood. Williams's thoughtful treatment of Christian education as discipleship formation offers an important element to the dialogue. Her historical review of the significance of the dynamics of formative culture and context of the early faith makes for a compelling reframing of what is most important in the life of discipleship: fostering a life of obedience.

Williams reminds us that the only essential confession of the community of faith was that the exalted one who was present in the community was the same as the historic Jesus of Galilee. All else was secondary. The goal of Christian discipleship was to live a life worthy of the calling to be Christian and to live in the community of faith. Against today's anxious measures of congregational success, the prophetic call of the church's measure of effectiveness in teaching and preaching is measured by the common life in community.

Williams states that she believes the hope for the church, and for its witness to the world, lies in its ability to nurture authentic discipleship. I agree, for that has always been true. But Christian educators will do well to appreciate that the Christian faith is acquired ("learned") in certain ways, and not in others. Clarity about the nature of faith, the nature of discipleship, the nature of the Christian teacher, and the uniqueness of the context in which faith and discipleship are nurtured is necessary for effective practices of educating in faith. Reclaiming the community of faith as the crucible for the formation of disciples is vital, for relationships in community mediate spiritual formation.

Important for congregational educators are these reminders: First, Christian discipleship is a way of life, not a program. There never has been, nor will be, an educational program that fosters spiritual growth apart from relationships in family and community. Second, Christian discipleship must be guided by tradition. To neglect or abandon tradition in favor of predilections, movements, fads, or marketing strategies is to risk crossing the line where a church ceases to be Christian. These essential points will challenge every pastor and educational program staff to stay grounded in authentic ways of teaching and learning the Way. It is so much easier to plan and pull off a program of study, but true Christian education for discipleship is the shaping of a person into being Christian, not merely doing Christian things.

Israel Galindo
Dean and Professor of Christian Education
Baptist Theological Seminary at Richmond
Richmond, Virginia

Acknowledgments

In 1977 I was a factory worker and spent my days seated at a machine winding fine wire onto little bobbins. Beside me sat a woman named Cathy Brewer, who spent her days soldering tiny crimps onto fine leads and who, despite the significant struggles of her day-to-day life, spoke of inner peace. On Christmas that year, my sister, Zoe, gave me a gift I hadn't requested but apparently yearned for in the depth of my being. Opening a small white box to find a soft-cover navy-blue Bible, I burst into dramatic and mystifying tears. I chose to begin my reading of this unfamiliar volume with the Gospel of Matthew. Through the Matthean narratives, I encountered Jesus and the grace of God. My life was changed forever.

The following January, I left the factory and night school to head off finally to "real" college. My first Thursday at Cortland State saw the inaugural meeting of a new campus Bible study. Slipping past my roommates with new blue Bible in hand, I ventured to the campus center, where I met Michael McKimmy and Ann Richardson (McKimmy). Michael's teaching and the kindness he and Ann showed engendered within me a love of Scripture and a new belief in myself—both of which gave me the courage to eventually pursue theological education. At seminary I studied hard, developed enduring friendships, and discovered new dreams, which culminated in my acceptance of a call to pastoral ministry.

After six years in the pastorate, I resumed my studies. At the Presbyterian School of Christian Education in Richmond, Virginia,

I had the privilege of working with Sara Little, a woman whose brilliant career is unsurpassed in the field of Christian education. In my first semester, I wrote a little paper titled "Education in the Primitive Christian Communities." Professor Little praised my effort with her comments, reading in part, "Hold on to this. You may want to build on it . . . or some publication opportunity may appear." Sara's gifts as an educator and her authentic care for her students (the two are inseparable) helped me to believe that I might actually have valuable contributions to make within my chosen field.

During that first semester of doctoral study, I met Chet Williams, a committed, intelligent seminary student whose profound struggles within the constraints of traditional teaching models forever changed how I view the educational process. That meeting also led to other significant life changes. In 1996, Chet became my husband and my most devoted fan, whose willingness to entertain my latest big idea knows no bounds. Whether by silently slipping in and out of my writing space to leave a cup of tea, tossing about ideas in intense conversation, or serving as my first reader, his contribution has been invaluable to the completion of this work.

I am indebted to all these people—family members, coworkers, friends, and teachers—and so many more who have nurtured my discipleship by helping to shape my life and support my dreams.

I offer a word of appreciation to my coworkers at National Ministries, American Baptist Churches USA, for their selfless encouragement, and to my manager, Marilyn Turner, and our executive director, Aidsand Wright-Riggins III, for the support and flexibility that has allowed me to pursue this opportunity.

I am thankful to the Alban Institute for so quickly reviewing and responding to my proposal. It seems like divine serendipity that twenty-six years after meeting her on the third floor of the Eastern Seminary dormitory, my friend Kristy Arnesen Pullen would advocate the publication of this book in her role as associate director of publishing at Alban. I am indebted to Beth Gaede, whose sheer competence inspired me to keep "pluggin' on" during the writing process, for being an ally, helping me to become a better writer and, teaching by example, a better editor for those with whom I work.

It is amazing to see how pockets and moments of my life intersect in the realization of this book. I could not have imagined or manufactured this junction. I am thankful to the Hand of Grace for this opportunity and to the community of the Gospel of Matthew, whose commitment to preserving and sharing the story of that very Hand of Grace opened my life to Jesus's love. I, like so many others who walk with Jesus in relative safety and comfort, owe a great debt to those first generations of Jesus followers for whom discipleship was costly and life changing. May we faithfully continue their witness to God's kingdom, and through that witness may our world continue to feel the touch of the man from Galilee.

Introduction

Pockets and Moments

When you feel the anguished desire for God to come near because you don't feel him present, then God is very close to your anguish. When are we going to understand that God is not only a God who gives happiness but that he tests our faithfulness in moments of affliction? It is then that prayer and religion have most merit: when one is faithful in spite of not feeling the Lord's presence.

—Archbishop Oscar Romero, from a Good Friday homily 1979[1]

It's 1973, and I'm in my small-town high-school history class. My teacher asks, "How many of you are Protestant?" About a third of the students raise their hands, and the teacher exclaims, "Wow, that many of you are Catholic!" Jump ahead thirty-six years. I'm having a conversation with a friend about her commitment to raising her children *outside* the church. She explains, "What intelligent person would possibly look to the church as a moral compass these days?"

Things have changed.

In the early 1970s a rural central-New-York history teacher could ask about religion and assume that most if not all of his students would be affiliated with the Christian church. That is not the case today. Contemporary Western culture is characterized by a religious diversity unknown in previous eras, but an even more dramatic change is an ever-increasing "unreligious diversity." Numerous folk have intentionally opted out of religion and have done so for a wide variety of reasons.[2] Few institutions are as affected by these changes as is the Christian church.

I have heard the sad songs intoned by our faith community: the laments of church folk over the decline of Sunday school and the absence of commitment, the dirges of denominational leaders about closing churches and diminishing resources, and the requiems of academicians who offer dire predictions and bewail the institution's having been disenfranchised by the culture. As a Christian and a church professional, I share that sorrow and suffer those worries. Yet I find myself yearning to cry out, "This is not a time to indulge ourselves in whining and worry!"

This is a time for repentance.

Repentance begins when we admit that we've lost our bearings, veered off the path. The church today seems to see itself as a victim of the culture. We complain that the culture doesn't give the church its proper place and that people have let the church down by not participating in church life. A victim mentality is crippling. It blinds us both to our role in our plight and to the possibilities that lie before us. I suspect that the church has become crippled by its sense of being victimized in our society. We need to ask, "Can the church be a victim?" Can the body of Christ, which is empowered and sustained by the very Spirit of God, really be *victimized* by cultural shifts?

Perhaps it would better make my point to turn the question around and ask, "Does the church need to be privileged to thrive?" Does the culture hold more power than the God who called the church into being? My suspicion is that the church has been so dependent on its privileged place within Western culture that it has lost some of its essence, its lifeblood, which flows not from an accommodating society but from the one who died on Calvary and rose again. I also suspect that the church is at least partially responsible for its current plight. My friend who has made the commitment to raise her children away from the church provides a vivid reminder that the church hasn't always been faithful to its calling. I think it is possible that our privileged place made us complacent and indifferent to our failings, and that those failings, in turn, have contributed to our loss of stature. If the church is a victim of anything, perhaps it is a victim of its own presumptions and heedlessness. We need to consider honestly our role in our current predicament if we are to be freed from the paralysis of a victim mentality and freed to embrace the possibilities that lie before us.

The second step of repentance is to take responsibility by turning from our old ways to embrace the hope that lies in a new beginning. I believe that this is a remarkable moment for the Christian faith, replete with possibilities. Within the former context of a church-friendly society, it was sometimes difficult to distinguish life-defining faith from comfortable religion. Against the backdrop of a "Christian" culture, it was challenging to live out Christianity as a phenomenon that creates radical community and *transcends* culture. Our current context provides a unique opportunity for us to shed the trappings of religion and "churchiness" and to dedicate ourselves to being communities of authentic disciples of Jesus.

At the 1998 annual meeting of the Association of Professors and Researchers in Religious Education, I attended a roundtable discussion about the future of the church. Responding to the question of where she saw hope for the future, Sara P. Little, distinguished professor of Christian education, explained that she imagined a future in which we would see arise small pockets of authentic, vibrant faith.[3] Professor Little's characterization reminded me of comments made by lay theologian William Stringfellow in the leadership tapes for his book *An Ethic for Christians and Other Aliens in a Strange Land*.[4] Stringfellow, an attorney who dedicated his life to serving poor blacks in Harlem, refers to the church as event rather than location. He calls us to consider honestly the history of the church in which we see not the static presence of the kingdom of God, but rather a transitory faithfulness, moments in which the church tangibly represents what the kingdom of God is like. He describes an institution of "here and there, and now and then authentic churchly character . . . not necessarily repeated in the same place or with the same people."

I confess that I have often found the church to be a bitter disappointment, whether as a poor, "unchurched" child who experienced the judgment and scorn of church folk or as the young pastor with naïve expectations whose days often ended in frustration and disillusionment. Borrowing the images of Little and Stringfellow and going in directions that likely exceed their intentions, I want to ask: Aren't pockets and moments of faithfulness what we see in the church, historically and currently? As we review contemporary and historic church life, there is so much to feel shame about; and yet, every once in a while, we see Christians acting in ways that make God's kingdom real in the world, moments that say to us, "You can do this too!"

This is a time for hope.

The realization of that hope depends on how we respond to the day. Responses to the challenges of the current age seem to take one of three forms. One response is to reject all traditions and foundations of the past as hypocritical, restrictive, intolerant, and unsophisticated and to embrace instead a wide-open future that has tolerance for everything—except for the traditions of the former days. A second response seeks to retreat from the trappings, styles, language, and mores of the present and to return uncritically to the "good old days" of the recent past. A third response is one of recovering and reclaiming our foundations and reinterpreting them in light of present-day realities. This is the response that shapes my approach to discipleship, a perspective that was born out of my experiences in the church.

TERMINOLOGY

I am using the concepts of Christian education, educational ministry, and discipleship formation interchangeably. I am aware of recent efforts to move away from the term *Christian education* because of a perceived narrowing of the concept to mean schooling, instruction, and/or Sunday school. Christian education is ancient terminology, appearing as early as 95 CE in the first Epistle of Clement, bishop of Rome, to the Corinthians. My hope is that, whether or not we can reclaim the terminology, we would reclaim the concept in its fullest sense. Recent decades have seen a preoccupation with changing terminology. Although adjusting terminology may move us in needed directions (for example, away from marginalization, toward expanded understandings), it can keep us distracted with continual discussion about wording and has led to an elitism among those who use the "right" language. I am working with a broad definition of Christian education as the ways in which Christian identity and lifestyle are formed, nurtured, and developed.

My calling to serve the church and my own repentance of a victim mentality require that I let go of my disappointments about the church. They require silencing my barren lamentations about how things are, and turning instead to embrace the lushness of opportunity that abounds in the present day. For me, as a Christian educator, that means wrestling with the question of how we can cultivate practices that nurture the emergence of pockets and moments of authentic discipleship within our communities of faith. The third response—that of recovery and reclamation—seems to me the most hopeful, the most connected to the essence of the faith while being open to a new day, and the most fitting for repentance.

The first section of this book is dedicated to recovering the foundations of discipleship by exploring the first three generations of Christianity, from about 30 CE to 130 CE. We will look to the faith communities that were emerging within Judaism and standing in the shadows of Roman oppression and Greek culture for guidance on how to nurture authentic followers of Jesus in our day. You see, before there was a religion called "Christianity," there were people who staked their very lives on the life, ministry, death, resurrection, and ongoing presence of Jesus. Before sanctuaries and belfries, before organs and offering plates, before pew cushions and stained glass, these followers gathered to celebrate and remember, and to learn more fully what it means to follow Jesus. Before Sunday school and vacation Bible school, before memory verses and flannel boards and even before the existence of a New Testament, there were formation, nurture, and instruction of believers within communities of faith. So we will start our explorations with visits to some of these "primitive Christian communities" and let them tell us a little bit about how they nurtured discipleship in the face of the challenges of their day. Once we've sojourned among the emerging Christian communities of the first century of the faith, we'll pause to gather up some insights from them to form general principles about discipleship formation. These principles will provide the shape of section 2, where we will unpack them in light of our current context. At the end of each chapter, readers will find exercises offered to help individuals or study groups interact with the material. It is my dream that by listening together to those communities of faith that lived and bred nascent Christian discipleship, we might begin to reclaim ministries of education that are vibrant, radical, formative, and transformative. It is my hope that the journey of listening and exploring will continue beyond these pages, so the book closes with an invitation to ongoing conversation.

DATE NOTATIONS

The initials BC have traditionally been used to indicate dates "before Christ" and AD (from the Latin *anno Domini)* for "in the year of our Lord. "This type of dating was introduced in the year 526 by Dionysius Exiguus, a monk who was assigned the task of creating a calendar for the feasts of the church. Misjudging Herod's reign, Dionysius fixed as the year of Jesus's birth the Roman year 754 (a few years too early) and used that date to designate the beginning of the Christian era. Some consider the use of CE (common era) and BCE (before the common era) to be disrespectful. This usage is becoming standard practice and shows respect for other traditions. I happily follow suit because it reminds us that (1) there are some things about Jesus that are misunderstood, even in the church, and (2) the things of our culture that we think honor our sacred story may very well misrepresent it.

I greatly appreciate this opportunity to share some of my ideas about how we might nurture followers of Jesus in the current age. I offer this book to faithful church people who are ready to embrace hope for the days ahead, and to the "dechurched," those who haven't lost faith in Jesus but for whom life in the local congregation has given way to cynicism and discouragement. This is a book for all who have the nagging sense that church has to be about more than choir rehearsals, chicken dinners, and disputes over carpet colors. It is for those who believe that Scripture can inform all aspects of personal and congregational life, including the process as well as the content of Christian education. It's for those who think the world is in desperate need of concrete witnesses to the power and presence of Jesus and who both suspect and hope, as I do, that revived and reformed ministries of education are central to reclaiming authentic faith and witness.

I also offer this book as the humblest of beginnings. I am profoundly aware that there is much more to say—and much *else* to say—on the subject of nurturing Christian discipleship. I don't imagine that I have conclusive or comprehensive answers, but I do hope to introduce ideas that will open up new avenues of thinking about what it means to be and to form followers of Jesus. So now, in preparation for the first leg of our shared journey, I encourage you to spend a little time with the exercises below.

Exercises for Individuals or Groups

1. Reflect on or discuss the local church and your experiences with it. The following questions may stimulate your thinking.
   - What has affected your involvement or lack of involvement in congregational life?
   - What aspects of church life formed within you a desire to follow Jesus?
   - How have things changed over the years in regard to the church and its place in society?
   - If you were asked to give an honest assessment of the Christian church, how would you rate its witness and faithfulness to Christ? And why?

2. Now, turn your attention to the experiences of others with the church.
   - Do you know people who reject the church? If so, what reasons do they give? Do you think their concerns are valid?
   - If you asked people outside the Christian church to assess its faithfulness and witness, what do you think they would say?

3. Which of these statements best describes your perspective?
   - I'm uncomfortable when I hear people critique the church.
   - I like how things are in the church right now; people just need to get committed.
   - I'm ready for a brand-new day without all the rules, myths, and strictures of the past.

- I'd give anything to return to the days when children prayed in school and Sunday was God's day.
- I think things should be different, but I'm not sure how.

4. Spend a few minutes pondering your current understandings of the beginnings of Christianity. Who was Jesus? What was his ministry about? How did you gain your knowledge of Jesus? What aspects of the Jesus story seem most important to you?

SECTION 1

Visiting Our Roots

In the three chapters that make up this section we will explore the roots of contemporary Christian discipleship as found in the ministry of Jesus and in the life of the early Christian communities. As we travel the eastern boundary of the ancient Roman Empire together, the question of how Christian discipleship was formed and nurtured will guide our inquiry. Some insights gained from our visits will be delineated at the end of each chapter, and these insights will form the basis for developing general principles for section 2.

In chapter 1, we will take a look at the ministry of Jesus, placing it in the context of the complex social, political, and religious world of first-century Palestine. We will be reminded of the Judaic background of Jesus's life and work; in particular, the centrality of the concept of the kingdom of God and the prophetic heritage that shaped not only his message, but also how he presented that message. Next, in chapters 2 and 3, we will visit with some of the faith communities of the first three generations of Christianity. We will look at what they had in common and the ways in which they diverged from one another. We'll note how they dealt with the challenges of changing contexts and increasing diversity within the family of Jesus followers. Ancient documents, especially the writings of our New Testament, will provide direction, but to find our way, we'll also need the guidance of others. We'll turn to Bible scholars, archaeologists, linguists, historians, and sociologists who have dedicated their lives to studying Christianity in its infancy and the documents that bear witness to the Jesus movement.

The story of the first Christian believers is, as are all stories from long ago, a complex one that necessitates wrapping our minds around times, places, and personalities quite different from our own. The chart that follows provides a snapshot of our itinerary. Some readers will find it a helpful advance organizer or a useful summary to refer to as we move along.

The First Three Generations of Christian Communities

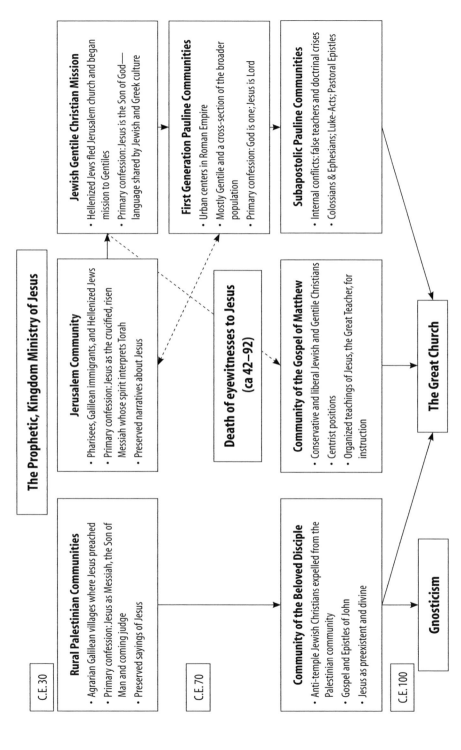

The Prophetic, Kingdom Ministry of Jesus

C.E. 30

Rural Palestinian Communities
· Agrarian Galilee villages where Jesus preached
· Primary confession: Jesus as Messiah, the Son of Man and coming judge
· Preserved sayings of Jesus

Jerusalem Community
· Pharisees, Galilean immigrants, and Hellenized Jews
· Primary confession: Jesus as the crucified, risen Messiah whose spirit interprets Torah
· Preserved narratives about Jesus

Jewish Gentile Christian Mission
· Hellenized Jews fled Jerusalem church and began mission to Gentiles
· Primary confession: Jesus is the Son of God—language shared by Jewish and Greek culture

First Generation Pauline Communities
· Urban centers in Roman Empire
· Mostly Gentile and a cross-section of the broader population
· Primary confession: God is one; Jesus is Lord

Subapostolic Pauline Communities
· Internal conflicts: false teachers and doctrinal crises
· Colossians & Ephesians; Luke-Acts; Pastoral Epistles

C.E. 70

Death of eyewitnesses to Jesus (ca 42–92)

Community of the Gospel of Matthew
· Conservative and liberal Jewish and Gentile Christians
· Centrist positions
· Organized teachings of Jesus, the Great Teacher, for instruction

Community of the Beloved Disciple
· Anti-temple Jewish Christians expelled from the Palestinian community
· Gospel and Epistles of John
· Jesus as preexistent and divine

C.E. 100

The Great Church

Gnosticism

1

How It Began

The Jesus Movement

Palestine was so strategically located that empire builders needed it, and required it secure, if they wished to rule the East. But because it was inhabited by a people with such a peculiar sense of itself—"You shall be my own possession among all people; for all the earth is mine, and you shall be to me a kingdom of priests and a holy nation" (Exod. 19:5–8)—Palestine was never a secure imperial possession. . . . Palestine was violently torn by political strife. So tense were the years of Jesus' ministry that his proclamation "the Kingdom of God is at hand" (Mark 1:15) could not help being both inflammatory and deeply ambiguous.

—LUKE T. JOHNSON, THE WRITINGS OF THE NEW TESTAMENT[1]

Christian discipleship began with the ministry of Jesus of Nazareth, who was born in Bethlehem in the province of Judea during the reign of Augustus Caesar and was put to death outside the city of Jerusalem when Pontius Pilate was prefect of Judea. Jesus's ministry was carried out in a particular geographical site and at a specific historical time. His message was formed by the legacy of Jewish religious and political history and informed by the particular social context of his day.

The Religious, Political, and Social Context of Jesus's Ministry

Aside from a brief period of independence, from the time of the Babylonian conquest in 587 BCE until the end of the Roman Empire, the Jews were ruled by the powers of the ancient world. Just sixty years before Jesus's birth, Palestine's century of independence ended in Roman occupation. Judea became a province of Rome, and the Jews joined the fifty million denizens of an empire that spread from Syria to Europe, throughout Spain, and into northern Africa. Herod the Great, Rome's appointed ruler of the province of Judea in Palestine, laid siege to the holy city of Jerusalem during the years 37 to 4 BCE. He implemented ambitious building projects and instituted excessively cruel policies toward the people. Palestine, a 150-mile stretch of land between the Mediterranean Sea and the Jordan River, which was the "promised land" captured by the twelve tribes of Israel, was an important land bridge between Africa and Asia, and formed the eastern edge of the Roman Empire. As an agrarian society, Palestine was inhabited primarily by subsistence-level farmers who were forced to support the Roman army and the urban elite of the empire through taxation and rent.

During the period of the Babylonian captivity (587 to 538 BCE) and thereafter, the Jewish faith had developed into various forms. By the first century CE, there were multiple factions or philosophies within Judaism. These factions shared belief in one true God who had given their ancestors the land of Canaan. They shared a sense of election as God's special people with the unique calling to manifest the kingdom (or rule) of God among them, as God explained to Moses following the exodus from Egypt:

> Now therefore, if you obey my voice and keep my covenant, you shall be my own possession out of all the peoples. Indeed, the whole earth is mine, but you shall be for me a priestly kingdom and a holy nation.
>
> —EXODUS 19:5–6

The foundation for this unique relationship and responsibility lay within Judaism's sacred Scriptures or Torah. In general, however, Jews in Jesus's day also held sacred the holy city and its temple, although different groups had different degrees of commitment to the temple cult.

Otherwise, Jewish groups of the first century had profound differences and were often in conflict with one another on a variety of issues and beliefs. For example, while the period of independence experienced under the Hasmoneans (163 to 63 BCE) engendered in many a hope for restoration of the Davidic line, not all shared messianic hopes that aligned political rule and the kingdom of God. Prominent among the sects of first-century Judaism are four mentioned in the Gospels and discussed by the Jewish historian Flavius Josephus. These are the Sadducees, the Pharisees, the Essenes, and followers of a fourth philosophy, who later became known as "Zealots." There were also scribes, who are frequently mentioned in the Gospels. These men held jobs within the local government and were often paid by the Pharisees and chief priests for legal advice.

PALESTINE IMMEDIATELY BEFORE THE TIME OF JESUS

From 175 to 163 BCE, Joseph, called "Maccabeus" (the hammer), the son of a priest, led his brothers and other Jews in revolt against the armies of Antiochus IV. Antiochus IV, who called himself "Epiphanes" (meaning "God manifest"), instituted a brutal policy of forced hellenization, outlawing rituals and practices that distinguished Jews from the rest of the society. He directly attacked the temple in Jerusalem, stripping it of its treasures, erecting a statue of Zeus, and sacrificing pigs on the altar. Those who chose death rather than conversion became known as *Hasidim* or "pious ones," from whom the Pharisees and other sects of Jesus's day were descended. The Maccabean revolt won independence, and from 163 to 63 BCE, Palestine was ruled by the Jewish Hasmonean dynasty. The major works of Flavius Josephus, a Jewish historian employed by the Roman Empire (*Antiquities of the Jews* and *The Jewish War*), provide valuable background information for understanding the political climate of first-century Palestine.

This was the world that Jesus entered: a world of political unrest, economic oppression, religious diversity, and tremendous social inequity. Jesus was also born into a religious heritage that inseparably intertwined religious and political reality. The "religious" law of ancient Israel was characterized not by individual moral codes, but by social constructs and a belief that the people's ultimate ruler was the God who had rescued their ancestors from slavery in Egypt. In ancient Israel, the temple and the court were situated in close proximity to one another. Priest and king stood side by side as God's representatives, and when things went awry, prophetic voices were raised to both throne and altar, calling the leaders and the people back to a proper relationship with God. The Romans were tolerant of individual religious practice but absolutely intolerant of political rebellion. Since religion and politics were inseparable within Judaism, Jews were considered a troublesome people within the empire. These historical religious foundations—a particular understanding of the reign of God, a commitment to prophetic witness, and intertwining of religious and political reality—shaped the identity and message of Jesus.[2]

Jesus as Prophet of the Kingdom

The writings of the New Testament present the life and ministry of Jesus from a variety of perspectives. We have four different Gospels, and even those called "synoptics," meaning "same view" (Mark, Matthew, and Luke), include different vignettes, emphases, and interpretations. The practice of looking at Jesus's life and ministry through various lenses, then, has the strongest of precedents. Additionally, the Gospels record both the primitive message of Jesus and the impact of that message on the early followers of Jesus, so we find in the Gospels the story of Jesus and the story of discipleship as understood by the primitive church.

The narratives of the inauguration of his ministry (Mark 1:14–16; Luke 4:14–21) reveal Jesus to be a practicing Jew whose his primary self-understanding is prophet and whose central message is the reign of God.

> When he came to Nazareth, where he had been brought up, he went to the synagogue on the sabbath day, as was his custom. He stood up to read, and the scroll of the prophet Isaiah was given to him. He unrolled the scroll and found the place where it was written:
>
> > "The Spirit of the Lord is upon me,
> > because he has anointed me
> > to bring good news to the poor.
> > He has sent me to proclaim release to the captives
> > and recovery of sight to the blind,
> > to let the oppressed go free,
> > to proclaim the year of the Lord's favor."
>
> And he rolled up the scroll, gave it back to the attendant, and sat down. The eyes of all in the synagogue were fixed on him. Then he began to say to them, "Today this scripture has been fulfilled in your hearing."
>
> —LUKE 4:16–21

Jesus's life and ministry were grounded in Judaism, its history, customs, sacred texts, and prophetic ethos. Reading from the scroll and proclaiming his very presence as the fulfillment of the prophet Isaiah's words, Jesus identifies himself with a long line of revered—and troublesome—charismatic leaders who, through word and deed, recalled the people to their identity as the people of God. Although history and faith have demonstrated his uniqueness, early in his ministry Jesus stood as one among others who sought to reform Judaism and to bring about social change. Not the least of these others, of course, was John the Baptist, whose influence on Jesus is well documented in the Gospels (Mark 1:9–11; Matt. 4:13–17; Luke 3:21–22).

As was the common practice of prophets, Jesus invited others to join his reform movement. There's an urgency to Jesus's summons

JESUS AND JOHN THE BAPTIST

Luke records that John the Baptist was the child of an older couple, the priest Zechariah and his wife, Elizabeth. His miraculous conception was indicative of his role in preparing the way for the Messiah (Luke 1:13–66). John was a prophet in the style of the Old Testament prophets, who spoke God's message in light of their contemporary situation. Prophets spoke about the immediate future, basing their prophecies on the evidence around them (for example, Assyria is about to conquer the Northern Kingdom), and about the distant future only in very general terms, usually offering words of hope that God would not forget his people. John preached in the wilderness, baptizing people in anticipation of a new work of God in Jesus (Matt. 3:1–12; Mark 1:4–8; and Luke 3:1–20). John proclaimed that the one who would come was more powerful than he, yet Jesus was among those whom he baptized (Matt. 4:13–16; Mark 1:9–11; and Luke 4:1–13).

According to the birth narrative of John found in Luke 1, Jesus and John were related (v. 36). It is likely that Jesus and John were familiar with one another prior to Jesus's baptism, and some scholars suggest that Jesus was a disciple of John and only began his ministry in earnest after John was executed.[3]

(Mark 1:16–20; Matt. 4:18–22; Luke 5:1–11; John 1:35–51) and his call is to a way of being.

> As Jesus passed along the Sea of Galilee, he saw Simon and his brother Andrew casting a net into the sea—for they were fishermen. And Jesus said to them, "Follow me and I will make you fish for people." And immediately they left their nets and followed him. As he went a little farther, he saw James son of Zebedee and his brother John, who were in their boat mending the nets. Immediately he called them; and they left their father Zebedee in the boat with the hired men, and followed him.
>
> —MARK 1:16–20

Andrew, Peter, John, and James leave their nets, their boats, their kinfolk—their very life definitions—and step into a new arena that will redefine where they go, what they do, with whom they eat . . . who they are. Jesus called his first disciples not individually, but two at a time. The call of Jesus was a call to follow him *in community*, to become part of an itinerant prophetic society that would carry the message of God's kingdom throughout the rural countryside of Galilee and eventually to Jerusalem, the center of Jewish religious and political power. In keeping with the prophets of old, Jesus conveyed his message in private instruction with his inner circle, through public encounters, and with prophetic symbolic acts.

Jesus, the Law, and the Pharisees

When we think of Jesus's public teaching, most of us immediately think of the familiar sermons and parables, which he shared with gatherings of people. There's another form of public instruction, however, that might be easily overlooked by twenty-first-century eyes. That is Jesus's debates with the Pharisees. Historically, the Pharisees have often been painted as the "bad guys," hypocrites who were in total opposition to Jesus. In fact, Jesus was probably closer in philosophy to the Pharisees than to the other religious groups of his day. He is frequently shown in the Gospels to be in the company of Pharisees, and Jesus counted among his friends Nicodemus (John 3:1; 19:39) and Joseph of Arimathea (Matt. 27:57; Mark 15:43; Luke 23:50–51), who were both Pharisees. Jesus seemed to know Pharisaism from the inside, well enough to be able to comment on how the Pharisees lived and to engage in robust discussions about their beliefs and their interpretations of the law.

For the Jews, the Law of Moses, with its protections for those on the fringes of society, its emphasis on justice, and its unwavering dedication to the sovereignty of God, served as a powerful contrast to Roman greed, oppression, and intoxication with power. The Pharisees saw adherence to the law as the means by which Jews could be united in faithfulness to their God even while being spread throughout the Judean countryside. The law, they believed, had been given as an expression of God's intention for the people, a symbol of God's grace, and a means for living in accord with the reign of God.

The Pharisees had developed elaborate systems of rules designed to unpack the law and to facilitate adherence among Jews throughout the empire. Heated debate over practical details of living out the Law of Moses was common among the Pharisees, and Jesus and his disciples seem frequently to find themselves engaged in such educational disputes. One example has to do with the matter of healing on the Sabbath, an issue that had not yet been settled among these teachers of the law.

> On the Sabbath, Jesus was having dinner in the home of an important Pharisee, and everyone was carefully watching Jesus. All of a sudden a man with swollen legs stood up in front of him. Jesus turned and asked the Pharisees and the teachers of the Law of Moses, "Is it right to heal on the Sabbath?" But they did not say a word.
>
> Jesus took hold of the man. Then he healed him and sent him away. Afterwards, Jesus asked the people, "If your son or ox falls into a well, wouldn't you pull him out right away, even on the Sabbath?"
>
> —LUKE 14:1–5 CEV

Jesus valued the law and stated that he had come not to do away with the law and the prophets, but to fulfill them (Matt. 5:17). In fact, Jesus advised his disciples to follow what the Pharisees taught them (Matt. 23:2–3). Jesus's argument with the Pharisees, therefore, appears to have been not about the principles, but about practical application and the failure of the religious leaders to heed their own teachings. According to Jesus, the Pharisaic missionary zeal for the law, which was intended to help Jews live faithfully, had the opposite effect. It became a burden and a barrier to faithful relationship with God. Jesus was about the business of revealing a better way.

Jesus and Prophetic-Symbolic Acts

In addition to public preaching, teaching and debating, and private instruction, Jesus engaged in actions that carried his message and revealed the kingdom. Some of these actions are referred to as "miracles" in the Gospels of Matthew, Mark, and Luke, and as "signs" in the Gospel of John. Others are simply dramatic activities that are noted by the Gospel writers, such as eating with tax collectors, welcoming women, cleansing the temple, and reinterpreting the Passover meal. The framework of prophet provides yet another way to view these dramatic actions of Jesus.

Jesus's actions revealed his power and confirmed that he was truly sent by God. They revealed the kingdom and supported his efforts to reform the faith. The question arises, however, why Jesus didn't do more miracles and just change everything. Why didn't he just heal everyone, raise everyone from the dead, or feed all hungry people everywhere? Why didn't he overpower the Romans and install a righteous regime, freeing everyone (and everything) from oppression? One possible answer is that Jesus's actions reflect a method of communication common to the prophetic stream within which Jesus identified himself. The prophets of ancient Israel frequently engaged in what have been dubbed "prophetic-symbolic acts" to disclose what God was about. An example provides the best way to get a handle on this concept, so let's consider one prophetic-symbolic act of my favorite Old Testament prophet, Jeremiah.

Like all prophets, Jeremiah was in the business of interpreting the events of his day in light of the people's relationship with God. Jeremiah lived at a time in history when only a small portion of what was once the nation of Israel remained—and this existence was tenuous. Judah, the last remaining segment of the twelve tribes, was at risk of being conquered by Babylon, the ruling power of the day. While some optimistic prophets advised the people that God would protect them no matter what, Jeremiah called the people to repent and warned them of impending doom. The people refused to listen to Jeremiah, and in the end, Judah fell and the major part of the population was carried off into Babylonian captivity. Jeremiah used words to interpret what God was about in those tragic historic events. He also used actions.

Later when I was in prison . . . Hanamel came just as the Lord had promised. And he said, "Please buy my field near Anathoth in the

territory of the Benjamin tribe. You have the right to buy it, and if
you do, it will stay in your family.

The Lord told me to buy it from Hanamel, and so I did.

—JEREMIAH 32:6–8 CEV

Why would God tell Jeremiah to buy the field just when Judah was
about to fall to the powers of Babylon? As the story continues, God
explains that even though Judah was going to be overcome and the
people scattered, someday their descendants would return to the land
of Canaan. Jeremiah would not see the return to the land. The generation that was toted off to the ends of the empire wouldn't see the return
either. However, God was not abandoning the people. Jeremiah acted out
the promise of God and hope for the future. Jeremiah's purchase of the
field was a prophetic-symbolic act. Through this act, he "spoke" God's
message and revealed what God was about in the history of his people.

Many of Jesus's actions can be viewed as prophetic-symbolic acts.
When Jesus healed, although he didn't heal everyone, he demonstrated
that God was at work offering wholeness to the world. When Jesus
performed nature miracles, such as calming the storm, he revealed
that in his ministry, God was reasserting divine rule over all of creation. When he fed the multitude and forgave sins, Jesus revealed the
kingdom coming on earth as it was in heaven. And when Jesus died on
the cross and rose from the grave, he revealed God at work bringing
life where death reigned.

In our efforts to understand and explain the momentous event
of Jesus's death and resurrection, we often inadvertently minimize it.
Theories of atonement explain the necessity of Jesus's death in terms
of appeasing God or paying for human sin. While it is clear from
Scripture that Jesus died for us, the ways in which we unpack that
concept frequently diminish both the need and the cost.

The fact that the son of God *died* demands that we (re)claim an
understanding of the depth and breadth of the impact of human sin.
The fallenness that Jesus addressed as prophet of the kingdom is profound and pervasive, affecting all of life and the entire created world. As
William Stringfellow described it:

Most Americans are grossly naïve or remarkably misinformed about the Fall. Even within the American churchly environment, there prevails too mean, too trivial, too narrow, too gullible a view of the biblical doctrine and description of the Fall. Especially within the churches there is a discounting of how the reality of fallenness (not the reality of evil, but the reality of fallenness: of loss of identity and of alienation, of basic disorientation and of death) afflicts the whole of Creation, not of human beings alone but also the principalities, the nations included.[4]

The risk we run when we adopt the language of Jesus dying for our sins is that, in our individualistic mind-set, we reduce sin and its effects to personal indiscretions and thereby minimize sin's effect and its cost to Jesus. Is the fact that I use a "bad word" when I feel angry or that a child tells a fib really a capital offense requiring the blood of an innocent? The death of Jesus compels us to recognize that we are talking about something much more profound and insidious than individual indiscretions. Likewise, the remedy of resurrection is devalued when

---

ATONEMENT

The word *atonement* appears infrequently in the New Testament and always in allusion to Old Testament usage (Rom. 3:25; Heb. 2:17; 1 John 2:2; 4:10), which presupposes the context of the temple sacrificial system. A variety of images are used to describe what Jesus does on our behalf. These include "reconciling the world to himself" (2 Cor. 5:19); becoming a "sacrifice that takes away our sins" (1 John 4:10); and setting us free from slavery to sin and giving us eternal life (Rom. 6:20–23). My interest is not in devaluing traditional images that describe what Jesus did on our behalf, but in challenging our adoption and explication of these images in ways that limit our understandings of sin and salvation to individual, human experience and thereby rob us of the cosmic depth and breadth of both.

we frame it solely in terms of individual salvation. Resurrection is the conquest of death by life and as such is a momentous occurrence that has universal and cosmic consequences. If we reduce sin to misdeeds and salvation to going to heaven, we demean the death and resurrection event and degrade discipleship, limiting it to a matter of eternal destination. Only if we accept the profundity of both sin and salvation are we able to embrace discipleship as a way of being that somehow continues the prophetic kingdom ministry of Jesus.

The death and resurrection of Jesus represents the ultimate prophetic-symbolic act. Even though, in his earthly ministry, Jesus succumbed to death, God, in Jesus, brought forth life, not bypassing death but moving through it and overcoming it. This act reveals the message that while humanity is languishing in death and visiting death on creation, God is at work conquering death with life.

As Jesus was revitalized, so too was the community of his followers, which had experienced a death of its own. At the cross, the community collapsed, and its members scattered, hid out, and lost all hope. With the appearance and sojourn of the resurrected Jesus among them, the community was resurrected and itself became the continuation of Jesus's prophetic-symbolic act. This was the postresurrection call to followers of Jesus—to be a community that revealed God at work in human history. In the next two chapters, we will visit with various segments of Jesus's followers and explore some of the various ways in which they lived out that call.

Some Insights from This Chapter

- Christian discipleship was born within Judaism.
- Human attempts to delineate faithfulness can actually interfere with the experience of grace.
- The call to discipleship is a call to a new way of being.
- The call to discipleship presumes community.
- The call to discipleship is a call to continue the prophetic-symbolic presence of Jesus.

Exercises for Individuals or Groups

1. Consider the following questions, either through group discussion, personal reflection, or journaling.
   - Are you comfortable with the concept of viewing Jesus's life and ministry through a variety of lenses? If not, how do you embrace the multifaceted witness of the four Gospels? If so, through what lens do you feel most comfortable viewing the ministry of Jesus: Messiah, Son of God, Savior, prophet . . . ?
   - What particular lens or lenses does your congregation favor, and how does that preference affect the ways in which your church nurtures discipleship?
2. Before you move on to chapter 2, spend some time thinking about (or discussing) the early church and the assumptions you bring to that topic. Consider, for example,
   - who made up the church,
   - what models for church life come to mind,
   - how and where the gospel spread, and
   - where you gained your current understanding of the early church.

2

In the Footsteps of Jesus

The First-Generation
Christian Communities

But how does it happen that the early years of Christianity are so shrouded in silence? The obscurity of the 30s and 40s can be emphasized by the comparative brilliancy of the 50s. For that latter decade we have the letters of the apostle Paul. . . . From them we receive the temptation to gloss speedily over the 30s and 40s and move swiftly to those better-documented 50s.

—JOHN DOMINICK CROSSAN, *THE BIRTH OF CHRISTIANITY*[1]

The companions of Jesus were faced with a crisis when he died. Without their leader, their community collapsed and its members succumbed to fear and hopelessness. That crisis was resolved through his resurrection and ongoing presence in the Spirit. A scattered and disheartened community of disciples was brought back to life by the risen Jesus, and with that renaissance came a commission. Jesus's followers were called to live out, as Jesus had, a prophetic-symbolic presence through which others could catch a glimpse of God's dream for the world. To fulfill that commission, those who had walked with Jesus resumed his ministry. They established communities of Jesus followers who represented not a religion distinct from Judaism, but a sect within Judaism. Often referred to as "apostolic churches" because of the presence of Jesus's eyewitnesses, these early communities were not planned, organized institutions. Instead they were spontaneous, enlivened assemblies of believers who were figuring it out as they went along. In this chapter we will make our way to the earliest apostolic communities, visiting first with those located in Palestine and then moving out to the first churches founded through the mission of the apostle Paul.

The Earliest Communities in Palestine

Christianity first took root in the city of Jerusalem and throughout rural Palestine, the heartland of Jewish religion and the homeland of Jesus. The appellation "Christianity" is a bit inaccurate, though, since the earliest Jesus followers were not actually called Christians. They were simply known as Jews, "Nazarenes" (Acts 24:5, 14), or followers of "the Way" (Acts 9:2; 18:25, 26; 19:9, 23; 22:4; 24:14, 22), a designation that likely reflects the itinerant ministry of Jesus and of the early Christian prophets. This way, which we now call Christianity, eventually expanded through the extended Jewish community to areas of the Roman Empire beyond Jerusalem and Palestine. In its earliest days, though, the "way of Jesus" was a phenomenon restricted to the city of Jerusalem and to small agrarian villages of rural Palestine.

Similarities among the Communities

Because the first Jesus followers were Jews, the early communities shared beliefs that echo the commonalities of Judaism as outlined in chapter 1. The most important shared foundational belief of the first-generation Christians was monotheism. While belief in one God may seem commonplace today, the centuries immediately preceding and following Jesus's ministry were only beginning to see a move away from localized polytheism toward an ethos that could entertain the claim of Judaism that there is a single divine being who rules the universe, has acted in history, and deserves humanity's solitary allegiance. Judaism's belief in one God was (and continues to be) expressed in the ancient creed or *Shema*, which was recited at the beginning of each synagogue service: "Hear, O Israel: The LORD is our God, the LORD alone" (Deut. 6:4).

A second foundation was a commitment to the Hebrew Scriptures, in particular to the sections known as the Law and the Prophets. There was also shared a commitment to the temple in Jerusalem; however, the communities reflected a diversity similar to that found in first-century Judaism in regard to the degree of importance they placed on the temple cult. Finally, all Jews longed for deliverance from Roman oppression, although again, there were differences in belief, especially related to how that deliverance would come. Many, but not all, anticipated divine intervention through a political liberator or Messiah who would rescue them in God's name.

The early Christian communities maintained the practices of Judaism until the destruction of the Jerusalem temple in 70 CE (Acts 2:46; 3:1; 5:12, 21, 42; Matt. 5:23). In addition to observing the temple rites, they continued with synagogue participation and family rituals, which included the recitation of eighteen prayers throughout the day. Their faith was woven into all aspects of life through annual, weekly, and daily worship and learning. They also gathered at private homes for formal prayer and teaching meetings and for informal fellowship meals. These gatherings maintained distinctly Jewish prayers and teaching from the Hebrew Scriptures. To these practices were added new elements, such as addressing God as Abba, reciting what we now call the Lord's Prayer, teaching the Jesus tradition, and sharing in the table fellowship of Jesus through a common meal.

No written documents are available from these earliest communities. It is commonly believed, though, that they were forming oral collections of the traditions of Jesus for use in proclamation, worship, and confrontation with opponents. Teaching the Hebrew Scriptures and the Jesus tradition involved both passing on and interpreting those traditions. Hymn singing at fellowship meals also played a role in sharing the faith traditions. Glimpses of these hymns, which reflect a belief that the Jewish Messiah had come, can be found within the Gospels.[2] For example, Luke places one such hymnic witness on the lips of Simeon:

> Master, now you are dismissing your servant in peace,
> according to your word;
> for my eyes have seen your salvation,
> which you have prepared in the presence of all peoples,
> a light for revelation to the Gentiles
> and for glory to your people Israel.
> —LUKE 2:29–32

While the earliest Palestinian communities had much in common, there were distinctions among them. There was even some dissension, as we will discover in our visits to the Jerusalem community, the rural Palestinian communities, and the Jewish Gentile Christian mission.

The Jerusalem Community

Jerusalem was the urban center of Palestine and the political and religious center of Judaism. Since farming wasn't possible in Jerusalem, the community was economically dependent on the temple and on the trade and tourism that came with the temple. Jerusalem was home to shopkeepers, lawyers, priestly families, and religious teachers. The community was conservative and traditional in the sense that it focused on the temple and on fulfillment of the Law of Moses or the *Torah*. The people were also politically and economically dependent on Rome. The temple stood in Jerusalem only as long as the empire allowed it to, and the citizens of the holy city may have been granted relief by Rome from the excessive taxation imposed on the rest of the empire.

The Jerusalem community of Jesus followers was a mixed group, made up of believing Pharisees, lower-class Galilean farmers and fishermen who had emigrated to Jerusalem, and Hellenists (Greek-named, Greek-speaking Jews) who had come to Jerusalem from remote areas of the Roman Empire. This community was distinguished by its communal lifestyle. It appears that the members were trying to fulfill a vision of the Messianic Age in which the presence of the crucified, risen Jesus transformed relationships and created a radically interdependent society. This cooperative, mutually supportive community is presented in Acts (2:43–47; 4:32–5:16) as a sign that validated the preaching of the gospel. There was, however, tension among the members, much of which reflected cultural distinctions and differences in beliefs.

The ministry of the Jerusalem community began as spontaneous and charismatic, relying on the Spirit and vision for direction, and then went through several stages of development. Initially leadership was structured around "the Twelve," which is both a reference to the apostles and a symbol of the twelve tribes of Israel. Among the Twelve were James, the son of Zebedee, who was beheaded in 42 CE, and his brother, John, who along with Peter gained prominence as a preacher and defender of the gospel to the broader Jewish community (Acts 3:1–4:22, 9–11). After some time, the role of the Twelve diminished, and leadership within the community appears to have come to rest on the pillars of the church (Gal. 2:9), which included Peter, John, the brothers of Jesus (James, Joseph, Simon, and Judas), and Jesus's mother, Mary. James was the oldest of Jesus's brothers, and he came into prominence in the Jerusalem community, which in turn exercised a degree of authority over the other Christian communities.[3] James was killed by Agrippa in 62 CE, and soon after, Peter and John faded into history, likely dying as martyrs for their preaching. The community eventually adopted the synagogue pattern (possibly put into place by James) of having ruling elders. Even with this somewhat rigid structure, which limited the charismatic authority that had prevailed in the nascent Jerusalem community, certain issues were brought to the entire membership (Gal. 2:2–5; Acts 15:22), and the Spirit was still seen as raising up prophetic voices (Acts 15:32; 21:10).

The principal understanding of Jesus in the Jerusalem community was Jesus as the suffering, crucified, and risen Messiah. This primary confession was reflected in the preaching of Peter and the other apostles:

> In this way God fulfilled what he had foretold through all the prophets, that his Messiah would suffer.
>
> —ACTS 3:18

> And every day in the temple and at home, they did not cease to teach and proclaim Jesus as the Messiah.
>
> —ACTS 5:42

The community further understood Jesus as the Messiah whose spirit interpreted Torah for them, a belief that reflected their emphasis on the law. It is thought that this community preserved stories about Jesus, especially those in which he is seen teaching and interpreting Torah.

TRADITIONS OF THE EARLY CHURCH

The Hebrew Scriptures or Tanakh are made up of three components: *Torah* (the Law), *Nevi'im* (the Prophets), and *Kethuvim* (the Writings). It wasn't until 90 CE that the Council of Jamnia defined the writings and finalized the canon of Hebrew Scriptures.

The oral Jesus tradition gathered by the early communities was foundational to the development of written records that were likely used as sources by the writers of the New Testament Gospels. Scholars have deduced that there was an early document that the writers of Matthew and Luke referred to as they developed their Gospels. They have dubbed this document "Q" (for the German *Quelle*, meaning "source") and propose that its foundation was the sayings of Jesus collected by the Palestinian communities.

The Hellenized Jews in the community, however, did not share the allegiance to the temple that was prominent in the community. Ultimately they did not fare well in Jerusalem, as is evidenced by the stoning of Stephen (note the Greek name), who had spoken on behalf of the Hellenistic widows (Acts 6–7) for the food distribution. Eventually the Hellenistic Jewish Christians fled to places as far away as Phoenicia, Cyprus, Cyrene, and Antioch. There they began a Jewish Gentile Christian mission (Acts 11:19–20), which we'll explore below.

Having inherited the structures and rituals of Judaism, the Jerusalem community demonstrated the power of early socialization. Discipleship was woven into all aspects of life, and just being a part of a believing family and community meant learning through participation. Openness to moving beyond existing understandings, however, was an essential component of this identity formation. Tradition was not only handed down, but also interpreted in light of the ministry and mission of Jesus, making the Jesus movement a new day within, rather than a break from, the community members' existing faith.

The Rural Palestinian Communities

Beyond the city of Jerusalem lay rural farm villages, which were at the mercy of powerful absentee landlords and suffered greatly under Roman oppression. In contrast to the inhabitants of Jerusalem, the village folk, who were descendants of Jews who had engaged in armed rebellion against Rome, carried the full burden of taxation. Although they traveled to Jerusalem for annual celebrations, they were neither economically dependent on nor as committed to the temple as was the Jerusalem community. It was in these rural communities that Jesus had carried out much of his ministry. After his death and resurrection, some of his former companions returned to the villages that Jesus had visited and there established loosely structured communities of Jesus followers. These itinerant prophets exercised authority through their teaching ministries. They also presided over baptisms as a ritual signifying entrance into the community.

The rural Palestinian communities shared with the Jerusalem community an understanding of Jesus as Messiah. They expressed this understanding, however, not in terms of Torah but in term of their experience of subjugation. They confessed Jesus as the messianic Son of Man (Mark 8:38–9:1) who would return to judge the world and free them from oppression. While the Jerusalem community gathered stories about Jesus, the rural Palestinian communities collected the sayings of Jesus.[4]

The rural Palestinian communities introduce us to the practice of reinterpreting traditional Jewish rituals in light of the Jesus movement. The ritual of baptism, which had been a sign of cleansing and repentance, became a rite of initiation through the ministry of the traveling Christian prophets—a practice also evidenced in the Jewish Gentile Christian mission and in the ministry of Paul (Rom. 6:2–11; Gal. 3:27).[5] These communities also demonstrate the formative power of being distinct from the larger society. Their belief in Jesus as the coming messianic judge—a belief that focused the community—also illustrates the identity-forming force of beliefs that connect with day-to-day experience. The primary confession of "Jesus, the Son of Man and coming judge" guided their instructional practices, in which they emphasized the practical sayings of Jesus and explored how to live in hope despite the hardships of daily life.

Jewish Gentile Christian Mission Churches

Very little direct information is available to us about the early mission to the Gentiles inaugurated by the Hellenistic Jews who left the Jerusalem church. We can, however, reconstruct some of that mission from what we read in Acts and the early writings of the apostle Paul. While sharing the story of Jesus within Judaism involved interpreting existing Jewish concepts in light of the ministry of Jesus, mission to Gentiles required additional strategies. The Jewish Christian mission to the Gentiles necessitated finding ways to cross cultural boundaries while maintaining the essence of the faith. At times, this meant introducing Hebrew concepts to non-Jews. For example, while the larger world may have been undergoing changes that readied people for monotheism, the universalistic monotheism that was foundational to Judaism was not a given among Gentiles.[6] The first step of sharing the gospel, therefore, was to proclaim belief in one God.

At other times sharing the gospel across cultural boundaries meant borrowing and reinterpreting concepts taken from the broader culture. Proclamation of Jesus as Messiah or Son of Man rested on the Jewish hope for a redeemer or rescuer. That expectation was not part of the Gentile mind-set. Non-Jews could, however, understand Jesus as the Son of God. The language of "Son of God" is found in the Hebrew Bible (Dan. 3:25) and in the writings of some marginal Jewish sects, and was understood by the Gospel writers in a variety of ways as a reference to Jesus (Mark 1:11; 3:11–12; 15:39; Matt. 1:10; Luke 2:26–35). The concept was also common in pagan religious belief, in which it referred to miracle workers who were endowed with divine powers. Although it reflected different original understandings, this shared language was reinterpreted and served to express belief in Jesus as one who was one with God. The shift of primary confession from "Jesus is Messiah," as found in the Jerusalem and Palestinian communities, to "Jesus is the Son of God" also signaled a shift of focus away from the future to the past and present. The Hebraic communities' messianic expectancy of the final exaltation of Jesus and future liberation of the people was replaced in the early Gentile churches with Jesus's divine sonship, which was established through his earthly obedience and which empowered the community to face the challenges of the day.

The early Jewish Gentile Christian mission reveals that the task of forming disciples beyond existing boundaries requires making choices about what is essential to the faith. It shows the necessity of teaching people new concepts and sometimes even new language to convey these essential beliefs. Yet the Gentile mission also demonstrates the importance of moving beyond the constraints of traditional language to find new and meaningful ways to express faith in Jesus.

The Pauline Communities

Christianity spread beyond Judaism and beyond Palestine into the urban centers of the empire largely through the mission of Paul and his entourage.[7] Much of what we know about the Pauline communities comes directly from the undisputed letters of Paul—Thessalonians, 1 and 2 Corinthians, Galatians, Romans, Philippians, and Philemon— that have been preserved in the Christian Bible. While the Gospels appear at the beginning of our New Testament, the books are not placed in the order they were written. Paul's letter to the Thessalonians was actually written earlier than any of the other New Testament writings. Although Paul did not begin, nor was he alone in, the mission to take the gospel to the Gentiles, he, along with his companions, did eventually become the primary face of that mission. The Christian communities that were founded by Paul were located in urban centers throughout the empire, such as Iconium, Derbe, and Attalia. These cities had significant Jewish communities that could serve as the springboards for sharing the gospel with the Gentile world. Paul's preaching, however, was not limited to Jewish religious sites. Paul and his coworkers did much of their work beyond the confines of Judaism and shared the gospel in marketplaces and other gathering spots.

Paul's authority as an apostle (Gal. 1:1, 15; 1 Cor. 9:1; 2 Cor. 10:13–16) lay in his dramatic conversion from persecutor to follower. His conversion and entrance into apostleship came as the result of an encounter he had with the risen Christ while he was headed to Damascus to arrest followers of the Way (Acts 9). The tradition that

Paul received from Christ was confirmed by the other apostles (Gal. 1:1–15, 2:7–9; 1 Cor. 9:1; 2 Cor. 1:13–16), and he sought to have his mission endorsed by the leaders of the Jerusalem church (Acts 15). As Christ's ambassador, Paul provided leadership to the communities he established through follow-up visits and letters. In addition to Paul's personal authority, he had a staff of disciples who traveled and followed up on his teaching in congregations. Although the Pauline Christian communities were largely Gentile, Paul brought to them key Jewish understandings, especially monotheism and the Jewish hope for a new age (1 and 2 Thess.; 1 Cor. 4:9, 15; Rom. 11:13–15). The communities were made up of a socioeconomic cross-section of the population (1 Cor. 5:4; Rom. 15:14), and since Christianity was not distinguished from Judaism by the Roman rulers, joining the Jesus movement meant casting one's lot with a hated minority within the empire.

The language and concepts of the Gentile world were adopted and adapted by those who shared the gospel beyond Judaism in light of belief in Jesus. In the Roman Empire, Lord was used in reference to Caesar, as an indication of his absolute power. "God is one; Christ is Lord" became the primary confession of the Pauline churches. This confession reflects a blending of Jewish monotheism with the re-defined cultural concept of lordship. The confession of Jesus as Lord incorporated belief in Jesus both as the coming judge and as the one exalted by God, a potentially comforting image to those for whom becoming a Christian meant leaving the mainstream to join a margin-alized group, thereby risking the ire of the powerful, self-designated lord, Caesar. It is in this confession and in the increasingly Gentile makeup of the communities that we see the seeds of a coming break of Christianity from its Jewish context.

Since believers often gathered in households, the homeowner held authority, secondary to Paul and his entourage, to guide the life of the community. The structure within the churches was flexible, with individuals performing functions as inspired by the Spirit. Commu-nity members were expected to learn from one another, and worship was Spirit-guided, with people spontaneously offering their gifts and sharing hymns. Beliefs were shared through instruction, ritual, confes-sions, and hymn singing.

Teaching in the Pauline churches was similar to that in the rural Palestinian and Jewish Gentile mission churches in that it was practical, "urging and encouraging" the people to lead lives worthy of the God who called them into his own kingdom and glory (1 Thess. 2:12). Any sharing of the tradition, therefore, included recognition that beliefs are manifested in daily life. While the rituals, such as baptism and table fellowship, were defined by belief, those rites also taught, reinforced, and interpreted the beliefs within the gathered community. Confessions of faith were confessions not of what Jesus did or said, but of his identity. In turn, these confessions served to give identity to the community—an identity that was built around the very presence of Jesus. The confessed belief "Jesus is Lord" manifested itself in a profoundly different way of being together, creating a community in which Jesus's presence obliterated the boundaries between rich and poor, Jew and Gentile, men and women (Gal. 3:28). Finally, hymns were spontaneous expressions of shared belief in Jesus, blending Jewish influence with Greek language. For example, Paul uses a hymn of the community to support his appeal for humility:

> who, though he was in the form of God,
> did not count equality with God
> as something to be exploited,
> but emptied himself,
> taking the form of a slave,
> being born in human likeness.
> And being found in human form,
> he humbled himself
> and became obedient to the point of death—
> even death on a cross.
> Therefore God also highly exalted him
> and gave him the name
> that is above every name,
> so that at the name of Jesus
> every knee should bend,
> in heaven and on earth and under the earth,
> and every tongue should confess
> that Jesus Christ is Lord,
> to the glory of God the Father.
> —Philippians 2:6–11

The early Pauline communities demonstrate the way in which casting one's lot with a marginalized group shapes identity. As in the Jerusalem community, we see the formative power of participating in a radically different community; in this case, one in which people from a wide range of social classes were expected to care for one another as family. As with the Jewish Gentile mission, sharing the gospel beyond the boundaries of Judaism required introducing fundamental but unfamiliar concepts to non-Jews, as well as giving distinctly Christian meaning to concepts from other cultures. We also begin to see one of the risks inherent in reframing the gospel for new settings—the risk of losing connection with the context that formed that gospel. Finally, the early Pauline churches offer us a way of measuring the efficacy of our efforts to teach the gospel: the effectiveness of sharing the message is revealed in the quality of the common life of the believers. Effective telling of the gospel transforms social, familial, and political structures.

The crisis of the original followers of Jesus was resolved when the risen Christ commissioned them to continue his prophetic-symbolic presence and equipped them with his Spirit. They fulfilled this mission in Jerusalem, in Palestine, and beyond by carrying the message of the gospel across geographic and cultural boundaries and establishing diverse communities of Jesus followers. Another crisis was looming, though. Those who expected Jesus to return within their lifetimes were disappointed. Those who had looked to the eyewitnesses of Jesus for leadership and teaching would soon lose those leaders and face the question, "How shall we continue without those who actually walked with him?" In the next chapter, we'll take a look at the various ways the second and third generations of Christians answered that question.

Some Insights from This Chapter

- While the communities share a common tradition, the application of that tradition differs among the communities. They have different primary understandings of Jesus and express these in language that has meaning for them; their confessions express Jesus's identity and presume his active presence in the community.

· The beliefs of the communities create a distinct way of being together, and life in the community forms Christian identity. This formative power is enhanced when the community is seen as distinct from or at variance with the prevailing society.

· Christian tradition is a living tradition, handed down and interpreted in light of new circumstances.

· The effectiveness of the preaching and teaching mission can be measured by the common life of the community.

· Christian belief connects with day-to-day experience, has practical import, and makes explicit demands on the lives of believers.

· Rituals are defined by and, in turn, teach foundational beliefs.

· Carrying Christian faith beyond Judaism:
  º can mean losing touch with the Jewish roots of Christianity,
  º requires identifying which components are essential,
  º necessitates introducing folks to unfamiliar language and concepts, and
  º involves using new language and adapting cultural concepts to express the truths of the gospel.

Exercises for Individuals or Groups

1. Spend some time in individual reflection and consider these questions:
   · What, if anything, strikes you about the earliest Christian communities?
   · Did any of the information excite you? Perplex you? Disturb you? What might these reactions tell you about your understandings, commitments, and expectations of Christian faith and Christian community?

2. The primary confession of Judaism was: "Hear, O Israel, the LORD is our God, the LORD alone" (Deut. 6:4). The primary confessions of the earliest communities included "Jesus is Messiah," "Jesus is the Son of God," and "Jesus is Lord." These confessions reflect truths about Jesus and also reflect the peculiar context of

the communities. Respond, through discussion, personal reflection, or journaling, to the questions below. (It might be helpful to review denominational documents or your church's confessions, covenant, or mission statement.)

- What is the primary confession of your church or denomination?
- To what extent does that confession reflect historic traditions about Jesus?
- How does that confession connect with your faith community's life situation?
- How well might that confession communicate to new generations?

3. Review the list of insights above and consider which, if any, might be helpful to your church or denomination.

3

When the Eyewitnesses Are Gone

The Second- and Third-Generation Christian Communities

> *If I live yet, it is for good, more love*
> *Through time to men: be nought but ashes here*
> *That keep awhile my semblance, who was John—*
> *Still, when they scatter, there is left on earth*
> *No one alive who knew (consider this!)*
> *—Saw with his eyes and handled with his hands*
> *That which was from the first, the Word of Life.*
> *How will it be when none more saith "I saw"?*
> —ROBERT BROWNING, "A DEATH IN THE DESERT"[1]

Jesus did not return before the apostles began to die. The Christian communities were, therefore, faced with the question of how to continue without the presence of eyewitnesses to his life and ministry. The urgency of this question was intensified by the continuation of external threats and, more important, by the rise of internal conflict. In the face of disappearing eyewitnesses, external threats, and internal conflict, the second- and third-generation communities took a variety of paths for survival—and for the nurturance of discipleship. In this chapter we will visit some of these "sub-apostolic communities,"[2] beginning with the Pauline communities, then moving on to the community of the beloved disciple (reflected in the Gospel and Epistles of John), and ending with the community that is reflected in the Gospel of Matthew.

The Pauline Communities

Whereas the first generation saw the rise of two basic patterns of community life—the ruling-elder structure of the Jerusalem community and the charismatic, nonhierarchical model of the Pauline churches—the last third of the century saw greater divergence in the structuring of community life. This diversity is apparent even among those communities that shared a Pauline heritage. In the three styles of community that are reflected in Colossians and Ephesians, the Pastoral Epistles (1 and 2 Timothy and Titus), and Luke/Acts are found three very different responses to the question, "How shall we continue?" These responses can be summarized, respectively, as a focus on an idealized vision of the church, an emphasis on continuity through the Spirit, and the development of structure. By its very nature, the third response, that of the rise of structure, which is apparent in the Pastoral Epistles, addresses the question of discipleship formation in a way that the other two do not. First and Second Timothy and Titus will, therefore, be the focus here; however, to avoid suggesting that increased structure was the only response among the communities that share a Pauline heritage, we need to spend a few moments with the communities that developed in other directions.

Colossians and Ephesians: The Triumph of the Church

Although significant minority scholarship attributes Colossians and Ephesians[3] to Paul, I am following the majority opinion that both were written in Paul's name by one of his disciples. In both letters, we find Paul's image of the church as the body of Christ developed into an idealized vision of the church (Col. 1:18, 24; 3:15; Eph. 1:22–23; 4:4–5). Unlike the style of community reflected in the Pastorals, as we shall see below, this understanding of the church is corporate but not institutional. The church is presented as an organic, growing entity in which the life of Christ himself is lived out.

Do not let anyone disqualify you, insisting on self-abasement and worship of angels, dwelling on visions, puffed up without cause by a human way of thinking, and not holding fast to the head, from whom the whole body, nourished and held together by its ligaments and sinews, grows with a growth that is from God.

—COLOSSIANS 2:18–19

Christ is the head of the body (Eph. 5:23), and it is the love between Christ and the church that nourishes and sustains the church. This approach places discipleship squarely and decisively within a cosmic, idealized view of Christian community. It holds that the church is central to God's master plan and, as such, was the goal of Christ's life. In this response, the church becomes personified, and love for the church is engendered as to a consecrated person whose holiness is not damaged by the sin of individual members.

The communities reflected in Colossians and Ephesians remind us that, even with the church's inherent frailty as a human institution, it remains an organism with a divine calling. The vision of the community is of an ideal church that is the body of Christ—not a team, not *like* a body, but the very presence of Christ in the world—and that forms disciples who withstand both internal conflict and external threats and who take seriously their roles as members of that body. For those of us who feel disillusioned by the church, these communities issue the reminder that our discipleship is a communal discipleship— delineated, fostered, and lived out in communion with other disciples.

Luke/Acts: The Triumph of Spiritual Pedigree

As indicated in their introductions (Luke 1:1–4; Acts 1:1–5), Luke and Acts make up a two-volume work that tells about the life of Jesus from his birth through his death, resurrection, ascension, and ongoing presence in the communities of his followers. Likely compiled about two decades after Paul's death by a missionary companion of Paul and directed toward Gentile mission churches spread throughout Asia Minor and Macedonia, Luke/Acts emphasizes continuity: between Israel and the ministry of Jesus and between the ministry of Jesus and the life of the church. This continuity is grounded in the activity of the

Spirit of God throughout history, as attested to in Stephen's speech before the high priest (Acts 7:1–53) and Peter's speech to the people in the temple when he is questioned about healing a lame man (Acts 3:11–4:22). The Spirit who was at work in creation (Gen. 1:2), empowered the leaders of Israel (Judg. 6:34; 1 Sam. 10:6–13), and raised up prophets (Isa. 61:1, Ezek. 2:2) is the same Spirit who impregnated Mary (Luke 1:35), anointed Jesus (Luke 3:22), and authorized the leaders of the early church (Acts 2:14–17; 4:8, 31; 6:3–5; 8:28; 13:2–9; and 20:2–18). In contrast to the Pastoral Epistles, in which the Spirit is attached to particular offices (as we will see below), in Luke/Acts the Spirit is seen directly guiding every essential step of the community, *as it had guided God's people throughout history.* To illustrate, consider the prayer of the community when Peter and John were threatened by the chief priests and leaders:

> Master, you created heaven and earth, the sea and everything in them. And by the Holy Spirit you spoke to our ancestor David. He was your servant, and you told him to say:
> "Why are all the Gentiles so furious?
> Why do people make foolish plans? . . ."
> . . . So make us brave enough to speak your message. Show your mighty power, as we heal people and work miracles and wonders in the name of your holy Servant, Jesus.
>
> —Acts 4:24–26, 29–30 CEV

This spiritual pedigree allowed the people to face confidently the challenges of the present by remembering the significance of their past—a past in which the Holy Spirit intervened for leaders such as Paul, Peter, and James. The question of how to continue in the face of difficult circumstances was resolved in a discipleship of triumphalism grounded in continuity, which allowed the communities to face the future in utter confidence that the Spirit would not let them down.

The community life reflected in Luke/Acts, with its historical spiritual pedigree, reveals discipleship that is grounded in history and is experienced as a continuation of God's acts from the beginning of time. It presents discipleship as a spiritual enterprise that is absolutely dependent on God. The triumphant discipleship of Luke/

Acts is wholehearted discipleship, steeped in prayer and proceeding in a boldness that comes only from the power of the Holy Spirit.

The Pastorals: The Triumph of Structure

First and Second Timothy and Titus have been designated as the "Pastoral Epistles" because they evidence a shift in concern from missionary expansion to the care of the established communities after their founders had moved on. While some scholars have argued for common authorship, my choice to group these letters together for discussion is a functional one, made because the content of the letters demonstrates a similar response to the changing times, albeit in communities that appear to be in different stages of development. In contrast to the idealized vision of the church, which guided the communities of the letters called Colossians and Ephesians, and the triumphant spiritual pedigree of the communities reflected in Luke/Acts, the letters of 1 and 2 Timothy and Titus tell the story of communities turning to structure, offices, and hierarchy as a way to face their challenges. Addressed primarily to individuals charged with the administration of local churches, these letters provide a more extensive view into the practical matters of nurturing discipleship than do the other writings associated with second- and third-generation Pauline communities.

In addition to dealing with the absence of eyewitnesses to Jesus and ongoing persecution, the communities of the Pastorals were plagued by a triad of related internal threats: false teachers (1 Tim. 1:30; 4:1), Judaizers (Titus 1:10–16) and doctrinal crises (1 Tim. 6:3). The development of structure was an effort to safeguard the tradition that had been given to them. Through the emerging offices, precreedal formulae, and rituals, the teachings they had received from Paul and his company would be handed down intact—and any false doctrines would effectively be quashed. The charismatic leadership through spiritual gifts that prevailed in the first-generation Pauline churches now gave way to institutionalization and a more closely defined role of the Holy Spirit. The Spirit, which in the early communities empowered activities, now sanctioned offices, such as deacon and overseer, or bishop. While little is known about the role of the deacon in the later Pauline communities, the letters contain details about the qualifications and role of bishop:

Church officials are in charge of God's work, and so they must also have a good reputation. They must not be bossy, quick-tempered, heavy drinkers, bullies, or dishonest in business. Instead they must be friendly to strangers and enjoy good things. They must also be sensible, fair, pure, and self-controlled. They must stick to the true message they were taught, so that their good teaching can help others and correct everyone who opposes it.

—Titus 1:7–9 cev (see also 1 Tim. 3:3–13)

The apostle Paul himself might very well not have met all the qualifications outlined in the Pastorals for an overseer of the church. The tasks of bishops, which included settling disputes in church polity and seeing to the education of the community, involved not only teaching but also censuring false teachers (1 Tim. 1:3; 4:6–11; Titus 5:11). The content of instruction appears to have been largely directives about church life and ethical behavior built on the Hebrew Scriptures (1 Tim. 2:13–15; 5:1:7–18; 2 Tim. 3:2–5; 15–17) and doctrines about Jesus (1 Tim. 2:5–6; 3:16; 2 Tim. 1:9–10; 2:12–13; Titus 2:11–15; 3:8–9).

During the first fifty years of Christianity, baptism was characterized by spontaneity and flexibility. It required a simple confession by the baptisand, such as "Jesus is Lord," immersion in the name of Jesus, and the laying on of hands. As structure and offices increased in importance in the second- and third-generation Pauline communities, so too did baptism and the celebration that eventually developed into the Eucharist. The rise of internal threats led to the crystallization of belief into more extensive precreedal summaries of faith, which may have accompanied expanded and redefined celebrations, for example:

There is only one God,
and Christ Jesus is the only one
who can bring us to God.
Jesus was truly human,
and he gave himself to rescue all of us.
God showed us this at the right time.

—1 Timothy 2:5–6 cev

The rise of structure within the communities, the teaching office of bishop, the emphasis on rituals of baptism and the Eucharist, and the development of summaries of faith reflect an increasingly intentional approach to Christian identity formation. When the absence of eyewitnesses led to confusion over what constituted authentic Christian belief, the communities of the Pastoral Epistles responded by developing a structure designed to preserve the apostolic heritage through faith formulations, official tradition-bound leaders, and censorship of false teachers.

The communities reflected in the Pastoral Epistles demonstrate the importance of structure and qualified teachers to safeguard our sacred tradition. They highlight the value of intentionality in nurturing followers of Jesus—an intentionality that includes increased emphasis on rituals of belonging—and suggest that the further we move in history away from the Jesus event, the more deliberate we need to be in our educational efforts. Further, these communities underscore the importance of being clear about what we believe and remind us that the parameters of Christian belief are necessitated as much by internal conflict as by external threats. The Pauline communities are not the only voices speaking to us from second- and third-generation Christianity, however. There were those within the broader Christian community who considered the rise of structure and hierarchy itself to be a threat. Chief among them is the community reflected in the Gospel and Epistles of John.

The Community of the Beloved Disciple

One of the most exciting aspects of New Testament writings in general and the Gospels in particular is that they offer a bi-level narration. As they tell the story of Jesus, they also tell the story of the communities that preserved that sacred narrative. The Gospels, then, reveal both the good news and the impact of that good news on a particular people at a particular point in history. We cannot describe any New Testament community without a degree of conjecture, and quite often it is the biblical text that is our primary source for any reconstruction. Thus the process is often a circular one: we search the text to define the community and then use that definition to help us interpret the text. Such reconstructions must therefore be approached with caution. We have an advantage with the community of the beloved disciple, however, since we have four documents that issued from that community: the Gospel of John and the three Johannine Epistles. Through painstaking review of these documents, noted New Testament scholar Raymond Brown proposed a hypothetical reconstruction of this community that has gained widespread support within the scholarly community.[4] The following outline draws on his work.

The roots of the Johannine community lie in Palestinian Christianity, whose membership was primarily Jews who had accepted Jesus as the Davidic Messiah, as an earthly leader designated through selection and obedience as God's own son. It is presumed that in the midst of a given community was a man who had known Jesus personally and had been a follower during Jesus's public ministry. Into this community entered a group of Jewish Christians who understood Jesus within a Mosaic framework, similar to that of the Samaritan tradition in which Moses was exalted as the unique revealer of the divine will, the one who had stood in the presence of God and then had brought the word of God down to the people below. This messianic understanding, coupled with an antitemple bias, allowed this group to win converts from among the Samaritans. The presence of this second group and its "top-down" messianic view triggered the development of an under-

---

SAMARITANS

The territory of Samaria was in the central region of Palestine, west of the Jordan River. The ancestors of the Samaritans were the survivors of the fall of the Northern Kingdom of Israel to Assyria in 721 BCE. According to 2 Kings 17, those survivors intermarried with non-Jews who were deported from other conquered areas. Having been cut off from mainstream Judaism for centuries, the Samaritans developed their own edition of the Torah and worshiped at their own temple on Mount Gerizim until it was destroyed in 128 BCE.

---

standing of Jesus as preexistent and divine—or a "high Christology," which reflects, in part, the personified divine Wisdom (Prov. 1:20–33 and Job 28:23–27). These developments led to debates with those in the community who saw the high, preexistent Christology as a threat to monotheism.

At the same time, Judaism in general was going through dramatic changes. A rebellion waged against Rome by Palestinian Jews in 66 CE ended seven years later with the mass suicide of Jewish loyalists at Masada and saw the annihilation of the Jewish state and the burning of the temple by Emperor Vespasian. In the years following this destruction, the remaining Jewish leaders worked to define a Judaism without the temple. Leading this effort was Yohanan ben Zakkai and the academy of Jewish leaders at Jamnia. The efforts to define the limits of Judaism included the formulation of a statement against heretics. Jews who claimed Jesus's superiority over Moses found themselves increasingly separated from Judaism, and the stage was set for bitter division and eventual expulsion of Jesus followers from the faith communities that had spawned them.

The group that held the high Christology in our proposed Jewish Christian community was eventually expelled and, having been alienated from its Jewish foundations, faced a theological crisis. Helping the people through their crisis was the one who had known Jesus personally and who eventually became known as the Beloved Disciple. This is the likely context for the development of the Gospel of John, in which the community's distinct understanding of Jesus is formalized: "In the beginning was the Word, and the Word was with God, and the Word was God" (John 1:1–2) and in which can be seen a lingering hope for healing within the community (John 10:16; 17:11).

The Gospel of John also reveals the community's response to the increasing institutionalization of other communities. As the second- and third-generation Pauline communities were identifying offices, setting standards for teachers, preserving tradition, and defining sacraments, the community of the Beloved Disciple was embracing the Spirit (John 14:15–17, 26; 16:13–14). The Spirit or *Paraclete* (meaning advocate or comforter) alone was the teacher who received the tradition from the Father, and who, as did Jesus, contemporized and contextualized that tradition for each time and place. The only requirement for receiving this living tradition was a loving relationship with Jesus. While no institutional requirements are given for baptism and eucharistic celebrations, the community's unique framing of these practices demonstrates its understanding of Jesus as the divine source of life who nourishes the individual:

> I am the bread of life. . . . This is the bread that comes down from heaven, so that one may eat of it and not die. I am the living bread that came down from heaven. Whoever eats of this bread will live forever; and the bread that I will give for the life of the world is my flesh.
>   —JOHN 6:48–51

Further, John's treatment of the celebration hints at disputes arising within the community over the nature of Jesus. John 6:54 actually reads: "Those who munch my flesh," rather than the common translation, "Those who eat this bread." There was developing within the community a group that emphasized Jesus's divinity to the exclusion of his humanity. The Johannine Epistles reveal efforts to correct this perspective and its related libertine lifestyle. With its sole reliance on the Spirit, the community had no creedal formula against which to test beliefs and no structures with which to settle disputes among those who claimed contradictory teachings from the Spirit. Eventually there was a split in the community, and the secessionists went down the road to Docetism and Gnosticism, two major and related heresies of the primitive church. The remaining group adopted a pastoral structure and was successful in preserving the Johannine heritage for the larger church. In particular, the distinct Johannine Christology became the prevailing "orthodox" understanding of Jesus in the church.

The community of the Beloved Disciple proclaims to us once more that the Christian tradition is a living tradition that must be contextualized and contemporized, but only under the guidance of the Holy Spirit. While the community's Spirit-led approach provides a corrective to those who might become overreliant on structure and official roles, their split and eventual absorption into the Great Church demonstrate the need for some structure to deal with internal challenges. This community provides a powerful example of the intimate

---

FIRST-CENTURY HERESY

The two Greek-influenced movements within early Christianity known as Docetism and Gnosticism had diverse manifestations. Docetism maintained that Jesus was pure spirit and only appeared to be physically human. Docetism was a commonly held belief within Gnostic Christianity. Essential to Gnosticism was the belief that salvation is gained through special knowledge given by the Spirit and possessed by an elite few.

By the mid-second century Docetic and Gnostic versions of the faith were considered heretical in contrast to the beliefs of the "Great Church" (also called "the church catholic" with lowercase "c"). The term *Great Church* was introduced by Ignatius in the second century and is currently used by scholars to designate the church of that century (in contrast to the "apostolic" and "post-apostolic" or "subapostolic" churches of the first century), which saw increasingly shared structure and creed, along with greater connectedness among the Christian communities.

---

connection between belief and lifestyle: the heretical understanding of Jesus held by those who denied Jesus's humanity manifested itself in libertine living. Finally, the rise of this secessionist group with its divinity-only understanding of Jesus alerts us to the fact that when a community is formed out of polemic, it runs the risk of being so divorced from its roots and so focused on a single doctrine that its belief system develops into apostasy.

In the communities we've visited so far, we have seen great diversity in belief and practice. The Jerusalem community's affection for the law and temple stands in contrast to the Hellenists and Gentile Christians who resisted both. In the Pastorals, we found a strong reliance on structure and a narrowed understanding of the role of the Holy Spirit. In contrast, the Johannine communities showed us an emphasis on the Spirit that rested in a nearly complete lack of structure and the development of a high Christology quite distinct from the view of Jesus present in the earliest Palestinian communities. In the last community on our itinerary, we find an intentional middle ground.

The Community of the Gospel of Matthew

Among the New Testament writings, the Gospel of Matthew presents the Jesus tradition within the most distinctly instructional framework. The Gospel, in fact, presents Jesus as the great teacher (5:17–20). Matthew reflects a mixed community of conservative and liberal Jewish and Gentile Christians in Antioch, where the apostle Paul had earlier lost his bid for a law-free version of the faith for Gentile Christians (Gal. 2:1 ff.). The community appears to have been closer in perspective to the Jerusalem church than to Paul. The writer, who is identified by majority scholarship as a Jewish Christian and possibly a former scribe, presents Jesus's life in the context of the law and the prophets. The Gospel presents what can be characterized as a mediating position—geographically, theologically, and ecclesiastically—and deals practically with church life by weaving the church's own history into the story of the life of Jesus. Located on the boundary between the Semitic and Graeco-Roman worlds, the community seems to have been struggling with Judaic identity, disruptive prophets, and the dangers of increasing structure and authority.

The Gospel of Matthew is directed toward those who hold authority within the community and insists on a centrist position on pressing issues, such as adherence to the law versus reliance on the Spirit, human authority versus freedom and dependence on Jesus, old ways versus new ways, and guarding tradition versus contextualizing and contemporizing the tradition. This mediating position is fulfilled through teachers who pass on and interpret the tradition but who, like Peter, embody the teaching of Jesus and never exercise authority apart from him.

> But you are not to be called rabbi, for you have one teacher, and you are all students. And call no one your father on earth, for you have one Father—the one in heaven. Nor are you to be called instructors, for you have one instructor, the Messiah.
>
> —MATTHEW 23:8–10

The overriding educational principle of the community of the Gospel of Matthew is the centrality of Jesus. He is the first teacher; the authority of all other teachers is secondary to and dependent on him. The task of any other teacher is to pass on the tradition of Jesus by embodying that tradition, and any interpretation is carried out in light of Jesus's principle of love.

The Gospel of Matthew presents the Jesus tradition arranged for instruction in the form of five great sermons. These sermons are commonly referred to as the Sermon on the Mount (Matt. 5–7), the Sermon on Mission (Matthew 10), the Sermon in Parable (Matthew 13), the Sermon on Church Order and Life (Matthew 18), and the Eschatological Sermon (Matthew 25–26). This material, however, is more than instructional fodder. Through the traditions of Jesus, Jesus becomes present to the community, and the tradition is the means through which he practices authority over those who teach within the community. It is unclear how structured and formalized the office and practice of teaching were in the Matthean community. Matthew 28:19 does seem to indicate that baptism preceded, rather than followed, any formal instruction of new members.

The instructional material found in the five great sermons frequently contrasts the moral standards of followers of Jesus with those of Pharisaic Judaism by interpreting Torah in light of Jesus's law of love. The Pharisees represented the only remaining functional sect of Judaism at the time of the writing of Matthew's Gospel. They had begun a movement to contemporize the essence of the Law of Moses by expounding on the law and developing an authoritative oral tradition. Jesus's phrasing "You have heard it said, . . . but I say to you" (Matt. 5:21, 27, 31, 33, 38, 43) refers not to the written Law of Moses, but to contemporized interpretations of the law, which in some cases had themselves become rigid rules and regulations. The common practice among religious groups of contrasting the beliefs of the community to those of the larger community from which it arose served not to engender rejection of the parent faith but rather to reinforce a distinct sense of identity among the members of the new community. In the Matthean community's mediating positions, we find both the increasing emphasis on structure and preservation that are apparent in the Pauline communities and the freedom of the Johannine community, balanced by safeguards that keep those elements from superseding the primary loving authority of Jesus, the great teacher.

The community of the Gospel of Matthew reminds us of the centrality of Jesus as our teacher and the final authority who is made present through the traditions as they are handed down. Further, the community reveals that the Jesus tradition is not only a living tradition, but also a lived tradition. Only as the tradition is embodied in the lives of individuals and the life of the community can it be interpreted in light of the overriding principle of love. Finally, the community demonstrates the power of distinctiveness to form disciples. Defining its beliefs over and against the predominant sect of Judaism helped to solidify the uniqueness of Christian identity.

Some Insights from This Chapter

- Changing contexts require changing strategies; churches will necessarily look different in different places and times, even when they share a common heritage.
- The actual presence of Jesus is central to all expressions of Christian community. This ongoing presence of Jesus is framed in a variety of ways; for example, as the head of the body, which is the church; as the ultimate teacher whose very presence is communicated through the Jesus tradition; and as the one who is present through his Spirit.
- Nurturing discipleship in new generations requires structure and summary statements of faith; however, that structure and the wording of those statements must be responsive to the Spirit and to the community's changing context.
- Both overreliance on structure and unfettered "spiritual" freedom can lead to elitism, division, and a narrowing of the tradition.
- Defining the faith community in contrast to the community from which it arose forms identity; however, when a new community is formed out of polemic, it risks a complete break with its heritage and increases the likelihood of developing heretical beliefs.

Exercises for Individuals or Groups

1. The second- and third-generation communities developed in light of changing contexts and internal dynamics. Spend some time
    *   assessing and defining your church's external context and internal dynamics. What is happening within and around your community?
    *   thinking about your church, perhaps reviewing church newsletters, bylaws, or mission statements. How has your church responded to internal and external changes? Is that approach effective? What are the strengths of that approach? The weaknesses?
2. Spend some time reflecting on the following questions:
    *   Which of the communities described in this chapter most appeals to you and why?
    *   What does your preference tell you about your personality, assumptions, and expectations of the church?
    *   Which of the communities least appeals to you, and why?
    *   What might your choice tell you about your personality, assumptions, and expectations of the church?
3. Review one or two of the community descriptions above, and try to discern what assumptions about discipleship and the formation of disciples lay beneath their choices. If you are working with a group, you may want to have one or two people work on each community. Consider or discuss the strengths and weaknesses you see in each approach.
4. Select one insight from the second- and third-generation communities (from the list above or that you noticed in the chapter) that you believe would benefit your church. Simply identify the insights. There is no need to defend, debate, or challenge opinions.

SECTION 2

Bringing It Home

In light of the preceding discussion, I offer the following four general principles, which will provide the overarching organization for this section.

- Christian discipleship is a way of being.
- Christian discipleship is grounded in vocation.
- Christian discipleship is nurtured within community.
- Christian discipleship is guided by tradition.

Admittedly, these overarching principles are not particularly profound. We might very well have arrived at them without the journey through first-century Christianity. The power of these principles for guiding Christian educational efforts is found in unpacking them in light of the compiled and collective witness of the earliest Christian communities.

By compiled and collective witness, I mean both bringing together the diverse perspectives of the communities into a fuller picture than that provided by any single witness, and allowing the fact that the communities had different understandings to bear its own witness. It is important to recognize that the witness of all the communities has been canonized. For example, I feel naturally drawn to the centrist positions of the Matthean community, but I can't forget that the community speaks to me alongside communities that represent the very extremes that are being mediated. If my personal affinities lead me to embrace—or to disallow—any of the approaches of the early communities (the Jerusalem cooperative, the Spirit-led Pauline and Johannine communities, or the rising structure of the communities represented in Colossians and Ephesians), I risk overlooking the collective witness that all human attempts at organizing the faith community will have strengths and weaknesses and that even the least functional approaches may have treasures to offer to the church at large.

Or while the church has historically privileged the top-down Christology of the Johannine community, we cannot ignore the voices of the early Palestinian communities that present an ascending Christology in which Jesus, the Davidic Messiah, "became" God's son through obedience (Mark 1:9–11) and by being raised up, exalted, and gifted with the Spirit (Acts 2:29–33). If, instead of "protecting" the integrity of the New Testament by imposing the high Christology of the community of the Beloved Disciple on the rest of the first-century communities, we instead embrace the collective witness, we will learn that (1) we all understand Jesus—and express that understanding—from within the limitations of who we are and (2) a multiview witness is necessary to point our human minds toward the full and wondrous nature of Jesus. Those who see our tradition as something in need of protection may feel uncomfortable with this compiled and collective approach. Yet accepting the Bible on its own terms, in its unity and its diversity, is essential to accepting its authority and appreciating its witness.

Having said all that, I must acknowledge that the following presentation cannot help being influenced by my biases. To proceed, I must *select and formulate* principles and *make choices* about organizing and expanding them. My choices about what to emphasize, what to combine, and what to overlook cannot avoid reflecting my own assumptions and interests. That unavoidable reality is part of the privilege and the responsibility of bringing our dynamic tradition to life in the context of our own experiences, hopes, disappointments, and dreams. It is my prayer that I have been open to the Spirit's guidance in my efforts.

4

A Way of Being

Of course, the spiritual concept of grace goes beyond "information" and "events" into a realm of relational mystery. . . . In receiving spiritual grace we understand that we not only seek but are sought, that we not only know but are known, that we not only love but are loved. Indeed, it is because we are sought and known and loved by grace that we are capable of seeking and knowing and loving.

—Parker Palmer, *To Know as We Are Known*[1]

Discipleship is a way of being. We might also use the phrase "way of life," but I prefer way of *being*, because this turn of phrase points to the reality that discipleship is about personal transformation. While we speak of a Christian lifestyle, there is a fundamental difference between being a Jesus follower and other lifestyles, which can mean anything from collecting stamps to following a diet plan. Discipleship does manifest itself in how we live; however, it is not about imposing on ourselves a set of "Christian guidelines." It is about opening ourselves up to a relationship that transforms our very being and thereby changes how we live. Lest I digress into one of those language debates that I disparaged in the introduction to this book, let me state unequivocally that I don't want to argue the phrasing per se. It is the concept that is essential, and for me, *way of being* reflects the idea that Christian discipleship grows from within and rests on a fundamental transformation of the *self*. This distinction between a way of life imposed from the outside and a way of being that flows from inner transformation is an essential distinction and one that highlights a fundamental flaw in how the church often goes about the business of nurturing discipleship.

If I try to be a Christian by adhering to external rules, guidelines, and demands, I can be successful in that endeavor for a period of time and in some areas of my life. People with more willpower than I will be able to follow this way of life for a longer periods of time and in more areas of their lives. Yet, since doing so relies on human resolve rather than on God's grace, the endeavor is arrogant, graceless, and doomed to failure. Likewise, if we teach discipleship as good Christian living, rather than nurture Christian *being*, we bypass grace and invite others into an enterprise that depends on strength of will. While the result may superficially and occasionally look like discipleship—that is, we may succeed in developing desired behaviors in certain areas of life—the process ultimately does not help transform people and often results in an internal battle between the will and the self. The result is a kind of disintegration of being, a division within ourselves. Paul recognized this phenomenon as he struggled to work out the relationship of the Christian to the Law:

> For we know that the law is spiritual; but I am of the flesh, sold into slavery under sin. I do not understand my own actions. For I do not do what I want, but I do the very thing I hate. Now if I do what I do not want, I agree that the law is good. But in fact it is no longer I that do it, but sin that dwells within me. For I know that nothing good dwells within me, that is, in my flesh. I can will what is right, but I cannot do it. For I do not do the good I want, but the evil I do not want is what I do. . . . Thanks be to God through Jesus Christ our Lord! So then, with my mind I am a slave to the law of God, but with my flesh I am a slave to the law of sin. . . . For the law of the Spirit of life in Christ Jesus has set you free from the law of sin and of death.
>
> —ROMANS 7:14–19, 25; 8:2

Paul's struggle over wanting to do what is right but not being able to do what is right is resolved through relationship with Jesus, which leads to liberation. A story may help illustrate the importance of this distinction for nurturing discipleship.

Some years ago an acquaintance of mine went through a dramatic change in her relationship with the church. She went from a life characterized by complete disregard for the faith to a life completely focused on the church. This change was triggered by her second marriage, to a local pastor, and presumably by an experience of new or renewed faith. One Sunday afternoon when her former husband arrived to pick up their son for a camping trip, he found his child sitting in the yard crying. The boy explained that he had been scolded by his mother for not giving correct answers in Sunday school that morning. The child's mother came out of the manse waving a yellow card and commanding, "Make sure he goes to Sunday school, and get the teacher to sign this form, or he won't get his Sunday-school attendance award." The teary-eyed child bade farewell to his anxious mother as he rode off with his annoyed father. The importance that "right answers" and Sunday-school attendance held for my friend suggested a focus on externals rather than on inner transformation.

As I visited with my acquaintance a few weeks later, she told me a story that she supposed demonstrated the good "Christian job" she was doing raising her son. Her new marriage meant moving her son into a blended family, and he went from being an only child to being the youngest of thirteen children. It also meant assigning the child household chores—a new experience for him. One evening after cleaning up the kitchen, the child had told his mother that as he rinsed the final plate from a very large sink full of dishes, he noticed a big pot on the stove. He had closed his eyes and, clasping soapy fingers, prayed that the pot might not be dirty. The punch line of his story was that the pot on the stove was clean and, boy, was he thankful! His mother giggled when she told me the story but explained that she'd taken care to advise her son that those are not the kinds of prayers he should be saying. The relationship with God that the child expressed through prayer—and sought to share with his mother—was "corrected" with rules about what we can and cannot say to God.

My acquaintance had always been a fairly rigid person with clear ideas about how things *should* be. I'm sad to recall that the Christianity she adopted seemed to mean replacing her previous set of rules with a different set of rules, albeit ones that were built around church and expressed in religious language. I'm sad that the attempt of her child to connect with her and her new priorities by sharing his story about answered prayer had ended in reprimand. I'm sad that her son was being taught a way of life dictated by shoulds and shouldn'ts (a religion he later rejected), rather than Christian discipleship as a transformed way of being made possible through God's love.

A Resurrected Way of Being

As we look to the first three generations of Christians, it is astonishing to see how dramatically many of their lives changed when they came to faith. Some left homes, vocations, and families. Others gave up social status to join a group of outcasts. Some, like Paul, went from being persecutors to experiencing persecution. Many faced imprisonment, torture, and death because of their faith. We noted in chapter 1 that the Roman government permitted religious diversity yet was ruthlessly intolerant of political diversity. The early communities, therefore, could have lived comfortably if they had stuck to the "religious" aspects of the faith and dropped those elements that were perceived to be political. If they had simply been following a system of rules, it might have been fairly easy for them to modify those rules to accommodate the empire. In fact, it seems doubtful that they could have withstood the struggles that confronted them with nothing more than an externally imposed lifestyle to sustain them. I propose that the first communities of Christian disciples were able to persist precisely because they were not living *by* externally imposed rules but were living *out* an internally (and eternally) nurtured way of being, which could withstand even the most significant challenges.

A key question for Christian education then becomes "How do we teach a way of being?" Or perhaps even, "*Can* we teach a way of being?" The word *teach* can be defined as imparting knowledge or causing to learn through example or experience.[2] Sharing information, modeling, and providing learning experiences are, in fact, legitimate parts of discipleship formation; however, they are not sufficient in themselves. The word *educate*, in contrast to *teach*, reflects a more live and learner-focused process. "Educate" comes from the Latin *educere* (*e*, meaning "out" and *ducere*, meaning "to lead") and was used as a specialized term meaning "to assist in the birth of a child."[3] *Educate* suggests a supportive endeavor that assists in bringing about new life. The question, then, for discipleship formation perhaps is better phrased as "How do we foster a new way of being?" To answer that question, we must first define the way of being that we hope to cultivate.

While there are many ways to characterize this way of being called Christian discipleship, it is best defined by the most definitive event of our faith—namely, the resurrection. The first three generations of Christian disciples all experienced the risen Christ, some through his physical presence prior to the ascension and the rest through the presence of his Spirit. The experience of the resurrected Christ changed not just how these people lived, but also who they were; for example, moving them from being people in bondage to being freed people, as Paul put it in the Romans passage quoted above: "For the law of the Spirit of life in Christ Jesus has set you free from the law of sin and of death" (8:2).

This phenomenon of identity transformation is attested to even in those communities that practiced adherence to the law. For example, the letter of James, whose practical emphasis has at times been viewed as contrary to Paul's "saved by grace" approach, intimates that Christian behavior is secondary to the transformative experience of grace: "Instead be humble and accept the message *that is planted in you to save you.* . . . My friends, if you have faith in our glorious Lord Jesus Christ, you won't treat some people better than others" (James 1:21; 2:1 CEV, emphasis added). As New Testament scholar Luke T. Johnson explains it, James's "contrast is not between faith and law but between the empty profession of religion and its living expression."[4]

Christian discipleship is, then, a *resurrected* way of being. As Jesus arose, so too do his followers. Those who follow Jesus live in the reality of the resurrection, even when death *appears* to be the ultimate power in the world. Jesus proclaimed, "I am the light for the world. Follow me, and you won't be walking in the dark. You will have the light that gives life" (John 8:12 CEV). To say that Christian discipleship is a resurrected way of being is to say that it issues forth new life, life in which we are freed from the power of death in all its manifestations. The resurrection of Jesus, which makes possible the resurrected life of discipleship, is the most profound revelation of God's grace. A resurrected way of being, therefore, is characterized by grace.

Living the Resurrection: A Graceful Life

I frequently find it disheartening to listen in on conversations at gatherings of church folk. These gatherings often seem to be microcosms of the world with an overlay of religious language. What I hear are recitations of busy schedules, discourses on worries, tales of accomplishments, stories of purchases—and lots and lots of chatter, much of which sounds compulsively self-focused. Beneath it all, I imagine I can hear the inner monologues: "I'm working hard—please value me"; "I'm feeling alone and afraid—make me feel safe"; "I'm doing important stuff—I matter; I really do"; "My children are successful—I *have* accomplished something with my life." "I have acquired so much—I must be important."

Much of our conversation betrays efforts at self-justification through hard work, achievement, and even material success. As such, our conversations belie the foundation of discipleship; namely, that we are justified by Christ. We don't need to, and in fact cannot, justify ourselves through activity, accomplishments, or acquisition. I am not advocating adding more "shoulds"—I should relax, I should live simply—to our already burdened hearts. I am advocating a resurrected way of being that is freed from the bondages of shame, fear, and worldliness; a life *graced* to be integrated, undriven, unencumbered, and empowered.

While some people act as though they don't think they have any personal failings and others act as though they think they are the very embodiment of personal failing, it is my contention that all of us are painfully aware of our flawed nature. We just have different ways of proceeding in the midst of that reality. Some of us are self-denigrating, "Oh, What a Worm Am I" folks. Others of us are inflated-ego, "I'll Bet You Think This Song Is about You" folks, and some of us toggle between the two. Yet each of us experiences in our own sinfulness a separation not only from God but from ourselves. In Jesus, God offers us atonement (at-one-ment)—the grace to be "at one" with God and with ourselves, no longer groveling in our sinfulness or pretending to be perfect—and the potential to be in renewed relationship with one another and the rest of creation. The power of death, as manifested in human failings, which threaten to "dis-integrate" us, is conquered by the grace of the resurrection, which makes possible an integrated way of being.

When my husband and I take our evening walks in the parking lot of our six-hundred-unit apartment complex, he checks out the cars and I check out their bumper stickers. I recently saw one that read, "Work hard. Pray hard." I think that motto demonstrates my point, not because of what it says, but because of what it doesn't say. Whenever I read it, I wonder, "Where's the grace?" The approach suggested by that bumper sticker seems to be manifested in the church, even or especially among church leaders. When I was a local-church pastor, I attended monthly support meetings of clergy in my association. One such meeting took place at a beautiful retreat center in north central Pennsylvania, a significant jaunt from my home in western New York State. Since our meetings were breakfast meetings, the pastor with whom I "carpooled" arrived early, and we set off into the cold predawn hour and rural byways on his little Kawasaki 250. After ninety minutes of clutching the passenger bar and balancing my feet against the foot pedals, I arrived, cramped and cold.

As we sat around the breakfast table, I became aware that I was rapidly consuming magnificent quantities of the exquisite homemade quiche that graced the table. I decided I needed to pause and attend to what was happening around me. One colleague was proudly sharing his recently published book. This milestone received only cursory attention as others in the group entered into a round of "what-important-things-I'm-doing" stories. Everyone was speaking at once and ignoring the newly published author's ongoing exposition. It seemed that everyone was attempting to establish his (my colleagues were all male) place in the pecking order of clergydom. I felt chilled and weary, not only in body but also in spirit. "Are we really this insecure?" I wondered. Even in this beautiful, peaceful setting, we couldn't still ourselves. I wasn't judging *them*. The only reason I hadn't joined in the competition was because I was too stuffed, cold, and exhausted to expend the energy. These were hardworking, kind, and generally supportive colleagues. They were doing important work, and many had accomplished wonderful things in their charges. The problem obviously didn't lie in the authenticity of their belief or the strength of their commitments. But all that good *doing* hadn't translated into a secure sense of *being*. I propose that the problem was (and is) the result of an approach to discipleship that functionally replaces grace with personal effort. Having been raised in a culture that values doing over being and in a church that tends to follow suit, my colleagues and I were prone to a drivenness that contradicted the grace we preached. I think a better bumper sticker than the one that said "Work hard. Pray hard" would read: "Drive your car. *Live* your life."

In addition to proving our worth through activity and achievement, we often try to justify our existence through material success. The church has, at various times and places, not only tolerated but even promoted this propensity. A most egregious example, of course, is the so-called success gospel by which preachers promise material success for those who live for God—and send money. The phenomenon is also apparent in subtler ways among mainstream Christians. Churches often count dollars and building expansions as signs of their value and God's favor. We offer blessings for new houses and celebrate extravaganzas called "weddings." Church people are frequently as caught up in fashion, appearances, and acquisition as is the general population. Life in this world has wonderful things to offer, and there is much to celebrate; however, a focus on earthly goods can entangle us in the world, as Jesus warned in his response to two brothers who were arguing over their inheritance:

> "And I will say to my soul, 'Soul, you have ample goods laid up for many years; relax, eat, drink, be merry.' But God said to him, 'You fool! This very night your life is being demanded of you. And the things you have prepared, whose will they be?' So it is with those who store up treasures for themselves but are not rich toward God."
>
> He said to his disciples, "Therefore I tell you, do not worry about your life, what you will eat, or about your body, what you will wear. For life is more than food, and the body more than clothing."
>
> —Luke 12:19–23

How quickly and easily life becomes encumbered when we pursue the American dream. Mortgages, interior décor, specialized lawn care, private schools, and nail-salon appointments all have a way of taking over our lives and consuming our time, energy, and financial resources.

The drive for these things does not necessarily indicate superficiality but rather reflects an inner lack that we seek to resolve by amassing what the culture holds dear. We are embarrassed if our neighbors have a new car and we drive old jalopies, as if our vehicles measure our worth. We function as though when we are able to acquire enough things, we will vanquish the pains of the past (or present). Just as with activity and achievement, acquisition can be a graceless attempt at self-justification. The indifferent, indiscriminate consumerism (as William Stringfellow termed it three decades ago) that characterizes our culture not only fetters us and entangles us in the world; it can also make us active participants in the world's disregard for others and for creation.

Grace makes possible a resurrected way of being. It frees us from efforts to justify ourselves by doing, achieving, and acquiring. It empowers us to be fully and simply conscious, integrated, undriven, and unencumbered human *beings*. The experience of grace also empowers us to offer grace to the world.

Living the Resurrection: A Gracious Life

Another bumper sticker that I see on our evening walks pleads, "God, please protect me from your followers." When I first read it, I laughed, because I got it. Then I cried—because I got it. The bumper sticker made me think of the old *Saturday Night Live* church-lady skits. While the *SNL* church lady may be a parody, the caricature points to the reality that the public voice of Christianity is often one of judgment. Church people frequently function in our society as the rule givers and guardians of morality, dedicated to censoring media, monitoring relationships, and controlling individual behavior. We freely speak *of* grace but seem to have a hard time *speaking* grace—to ourselves, to one another, and to the world.

In the Matthean catechesis known as The Sermon on the Mount, Jesus is shown admonishing his followers to avoid judging others: "Do not judge, so that you may not be judged. For with the judgment you make you will be judged, and the measure you give will be the measure you get" (Matt. 7:1–2). This admonition reflects the truism that the matters about which we are most judgmental toward others are often the issues we ourselves struggle with. Consider, for example, the number of outspoken critics of sexual immorality who have later been discovered to be living double lives in that regard. While these folk represent extreme examples, the tendency to judge others by standards we fail to adhere to ourselves does almost seem to be an epidemic in the Christian church. In my experience as a pastor I became accustomed to the ironic turn of events—such as the time the director of a local drug-abuse prevention program went into treatment for alcoholism, the occasion when the deacon who crusaded against premarital sex impregnated his son's teenage girlfriend, or the discovery that the pastor who advocated spanking children for stealing turned a blind eye to the landlord who took advantage of families on public assistance because he was a dedicated giver to the church. The resurrected life, on the other hand, by freeing us from the shame of our personal failings, empowers us to be gracious; to speak to the world's desperate need not for judgment but for grace. Grace allows us to live the resurrection—that is, to live openly, honestly, confidently, and lovingly in this world, offering life in the midst of the world's bondage to the power of death.

One subtle yet pervasive way in which we speak judgment is in the boundaries we set around access to salvation. My commitment to Christ formally began one autumn, when, at age twenty-one and during a personal crisis, I started attending a nearby Episcopal church. The following January, I set off for college and there, eager to continue my quest to know God, I joined a newly formed Bible study. Midway through the semester, I received a phone call from my then fiancé, in which he excitedly proclaimed, "I'm saved!" I spent my summer break visiting him, and during that visit, I just couldn't convince him of my own salvation because I hadn't prayed what he called the "Sinner's Prayer." Finally, during one extended altar call at his church, I went forward and was led by a deacon in a petition to God for salvation. I wrote to my pastor back home of this news. His reply was that he'd never doubted my commitment to Christ and he wondered if perhaps I'd yielded to the pressure of the context. He was right, of course. I had a preexisting commitment to Christ. I had experienced forgiveness and was saved, but the narrow understanding of how, when, and by what language one enters into relationship with Jesus had spoken judgment to me, and I had succumbed. (Thank God for forgiveness!)

The traditional Sinner's Prayer demands that we enter the faith from a single point of need—recognition of sinfulness—and with a single understanding of Jesus: the forgiver of sins. It wasn't until recently that I realized that the coercive and "magical" evangelistic efforts I had encountered that summer were just an extreme example of what many of us do. We often insist that people can come to relationship with Jesus only according to *our* concepts, *our* experiences, and *our* expectations. By contrast, in our visits to the early Christian communities, we saw approaches to sharing Jesus that fit people's contexts. For the Palestinian communities, the starting point was the need for a rescuer from their day-to-day experience of oppression and injustice. That need was answered in Jesus, the messianic teacher of the law and the coming judge. In the early Pauline communities, the need was for freedom from the confusion of polytheism and from servitude to a capricious human lord. The answer to that need was found in Jesus, the one true Lord and incarnation of the benevolent Creator. Consider, for example, Paul's experience in Athens:

> For as I went through the city and looked carefully at the objects of your worship, I found among them an altar with the inscription, "To an unknown god." What therefore you worship as unknown, this I proclaim to you. The God who made the world and everything in it, he who is Lord of heaven and earth, does not live in shrines made by human hands, nor is he served by human hands, as though he needed anything, since he himself gives to all mortals life and breath and all things.
>
> —Acts 17:23–25

Paul presents a responsive gospel, one that meets the people at their point of need, which, in the case of the Athenians, was indicated by their homage to an unknown god. Our task is not to replicate any of the specific modes presented in the life of the early communities, but to heed their collective witness that a responsive gospel allows for multiple points of entry into relationship with Jesus—points of entry that reflect the various contexts of human life. When we insist that the experience of discipleship must necessarily begin for others exactly as it began for us, we are judging those who don't share our particular words, concepts, and experiences. A resurrected way of being doesn't monitor how people become Christians. It speaks grace—a language that is nonjudgmental and contextual—and celebrates the diverse and manifold ways in which people open themselves up to relationship with Jesus.

The Starting Point of Christian Education

Christian discipleship is a way of being that begins and ends with grace. The impact of any Christian endeavor is diminished if our efforts flow out of insecure, driven, demanding, and graceless lives. We cannot teach what we do not know. And we cannot help teaching what we do know. Grace begets resurrected lives, and being able to assist effectively in the birthing process of discipleship means continually cultivating our own experiences of grace. This understanding is in keeping with educator and author Parker Palmer's characterization of teaching in general:

> So the transformation of teaching must begin in the transformed heart of the teacher. Only in the heart searched and transformed by truth will new teaching techniques and strategies for institutional change find sure grounding.[5]

Nurturing discipleship requires teachers with transformed hearts: teachers who live resurrected lives and speak the language of grace.

The resurrection of Jesus spoke life in the midst of death—this is the language of grace. We all learn to speak grace as a second language because grace is not the *lingua franca* of fallen humanity. Outlined below are some suggested practices for learning grace as a second language. Because these are *practices*, care needs to be taken lest we adopt them as rigid rules to be obeyed. These are tools for self-nurturing that can help us to internalize the language of grace and to move toward fluency. You may find that all, some, or none of these work well for you. You may discover other practices that are more effective for you. That is all OK. If, however, you find that you are turning these practices into oppressive external demands, you would do better to dance a jig, fly a kite, or eat some chocolate.

Awareness

Resurrected life demands consciousness—of who we are, what we feel, and what's happening around us. While it may seem a simple thing, it can be difficult to practice awareness. Most of us have been bred to be people pleasers and therefore are so tuned in to what others want from us that it takes effort to assess honestly and accurately what we desire, feel, see, and think, and then it takes courage to be honest about those things. Many of us are also so schooled in how things *should* be that we find it difficult to admit how things actually are, but our hope—the hope of the church, and the hope for the world—lies in open-eyed, honest assessment of the reality of our situation. In the words of William Stringfellow, Christian hope is realism:

> The beginning of hope is, for biblical people, full and relentless realism about the world as it is. . . . Any view that is less than realistic ends in understatement of the truth, and in illusion—if not delusion—with regard to hope; ends in false hopes, in hopes that betray us, in futile hopes. The message of the gospel is a real hope. It speaks of resurrection from the dead, resurrection from the power of death—freedom and transcendence of the power of death in its fullness, awesomeness, in its pervasiveness and diversity in the everyday life of the world.[6]

We cannot begin to know where we need to go or how to get there unless we are "relentlessly realistic" about where we are. Practicing consciousness allows us to assess our current situation honestly and provides us with the information we need to be deliberate in our efforts to experience and use the language of grace.

Listening

The language of grace emanates from God as its creator and native speaker, so we need to listen for God's voice to learn this language. God spoke grace in the act of creating and giving us life. God speaks grace even, or perhaps especially, in the midst of the disasters of human history. During the psalmist's imaginings of the worst—the breakdown of the natural world and the collapse of nations—he hears the voice of God speaking grace: "Be still and know that I am God!" (Ps. 46:10). When we calm our bodies, quiet our tongues, and settle our minds, we can hear God's voice in the stillness. God has spoken grace most powerfully in offering us new life through the ministry, death, and resurrection of Jesus. Spending time focused in silence on the cross or imagining the touch of Jesus can instill in us the vocabulary of divine love. Some would call this practice prayer or meditation. Whatever the terminology, as with all the spiritual disciplines the goal of this practice is to make us receptive to the language of grace, as Parker Palmer notes:

> The disciplines of spiritual formation aim finally at enlarging our capacity to receive this grace, a grace that is always reaching for us from the heart of love. It is a gift we cannot manipulate and command but for which we can only pray.[7]

We can learn to speak the language of grace only if we quiet the vernacular that prattles through our weary brains so that we can listen to the One who speaks grace with every breath.

Immersion

Fluency in any language is enhanced when we immerse ourselves in venues where the language can be heard. Grace can be heard within authentic Christian community and in the church's sacred tradition as expressed in Scripture, creedal summaries, hymns, artwork, symbols, and rituals. "The heavens are telling the glory of God," proclaims Psalm 19, reminding us that the language of the Creator can also be heard in creation. Even in the midst of fallenness, articulations of grace are present in the whistle of the wind, the song of the brook, and the trill of the willet.

In our technological age, time itself has become a prop in the stage production of our lives. We manipulate time to suit our schedules. Electricity banishes the night, making it possible for us to shop, work, and play twenty-four hours a day. TiVo, DVD-Rs, and "on-demand" programming free us from having to plan around the broadcast times of our favorite shows. Nature is one of the few remaining entities that demand we live in real time.

The office complex where I work is adorned with tulip trees that blossom into a magical wonderland each spring. This year I was away from the office for a three-week span during which the blooms flourished and then withered. I missed the wonderland. Nature would not wait on my schedule. Creation forces us to be present in the moment if we want to appreciate its offerings, and that requirement is itself a gift. When we turn our ears to the voice of creation, we hear the gracious call to *be*—right now, in the present moment, just as we are—and to know that the One who created every natural wonder also created us. Immersing ourselves in nature's communications can help us replace our harried tongue with the language of grace, which is our rightful heritage as members of the created order.

Practice

Try speaking the words *resurrection, grace, life*. How does that feel? I experience speaking those words as expanding and uplifting, and perhaps you have the same response. Now say "should." "I should do this." "You should not have done that." How does that feel? Perhaps like me, you find that using "should" language feels constricting and heavy. "Should" does not exist in the vocabulary of grace, but if we were to delete the word from church life—from Sunday-school lessons, sermons, church meetings, and churchgoing-family discussions—we could make lots of room to accommodate the words and phases of grace.

We cannot become fluent in grace unless we are courageous enough to try it out, to experiment with different phrases and learn what works and what doesn't. We might feel odd using phrases of love, acceptance, and support. People, especially those who are accustomed to hearing the language of judgment coming from our clan, might be a bit confused by this new dialect. Such awkwardness is evidence of how reliant we are on graceless language. Yet intentional practice of a second language is the way for it to become second nature to us—and comfortingly familiar to those who listen to us.

Practicing the language of grace also includes speaking it to ourselves, replacing that inner monologue of judgment with words

DISCIPLE, DISCIPLINES, AND DISCIPLINE

While some of the practices I propose reflect classic spiritual disciplines, I have opted not to call them "disciplines" because of the term's sometimes coercive connotations. A troublesome use of the term _discipline_ refers to punishment of children. Some people speak, even of hitting children, as "discipline," which is designed to "teach a lesson"! What occurs when a child is hit is neither discipline nor teaching, although children may inadvertently learn some things from corporal punishment—fear of adults, self-loathing, and violence as an acceptable way to treat others. This coercive sense is also present in the frequent claim of Christian leaders that "'Discipleship' comes from the word _discipline_," which suggests that discipleship is about enforced discipline (on self or another). Etymologically _disciple_ and _discipline_ both come from the Latin _discere_, which means "to learn." According to the _Illustrated Dictionary and Concordance of the Bible_, "disciple" means learner, and it is used in the Gospels in reference to both an exclusive group of people who were close to Jesus and also to all who respond to Jesus, designating "the condition of being followers of Jesus."[8] Rather than define _disciple_ through recourse to "discipline," we might better define _discipline_ through recourse to "disciple," which supports the notion of discipleship as a way of being that flows from relationship with Jesus.

of gentleness and self-acceptance. And finally, high-quality practice requires taking care not to listen to those who pretend to speak the language but don't really know it: the woman who promises to pray that your teenager learns some manners or the worship leader who praises God that you finally showed up at church. Time spent with those who misuse the language will lead to confusion and bad habits. There's a good possibility, however, that those who speak a false language of grace might listen in to our practice and learn a few things from us.

It is important to keep in mind that the language of grace exists whether we feel it or not. It may even be most important to listen for the language and practice it when it feels like a myth. However, even if we don't practice it, hear it, or believe in it, the language of grace remains real. It is the language that Jesus spoke so eloquently from the cross. It is the language that invites us into discipleship. And it is the language spoken by the very creator of language itself.

Exercises for Individuals or Groups

1. Think about how you first connected with Jesus. You may want to relive your early experiences of connecting with Jesus through writing or drawing. Consider or discuss what your experience has to say about nurturing discipleship in others.
2. Develop a license-plate motto that succinctly expresses your understanding of Christian discipleship as a way of being.
3. Think of a time when you heard the language of grace. What were the circumstances? Who spoke it to you? What was the impact on you?
4. Make a list with two columns—one of gracious words and phrases and the other of ungracious words and phrases. Covenant with another person or group to practice intentionally replacing ungracious language with the gracious phrases you have identified.
5. Name the ways your church does or doesn't speak the language of grace. What practices might help you and your church increase fluency in this language?

5

Grounded in Vocation

Christianity begins from and finally depends on the conviction that in Jesus we still have a paradigm for our relationship to God and to one another, that in Jesus' life, death and life out of death we see the clearest and fullest embodiment of divine grace, of creative wisdom and power, that ever achieved historical actuality, that Christians are accepted by God and enabled to love God and their neighbours by that same grace which we now recognize to have the same character of that same Jesus.

—JAMES D. G. DUNN, *UNITY AND DIVERSITY IN THE NEW TESTAMENT*[1]

Christian discipleship began with vocation, with the "call" (from the Latin *vocare*) of Jesus to some fishermen. Jesus's call was a call to relationship: "Come, follow *me*." After exploring beliefs about Jesus among the earliest Christians, noted New Testament scholar James Dunn arrived at the conclusion that in the midst of their tremendous diversity, these first-century communities held one thing in common: "the *exaltation* of the man Jesus and a *continuity* between Jesus of Nazareth and the one who enabled them to come to God."[2] Whether among first-generation Jewish followers of the Way, third-generation Gentile Christians in Asia Minor, or twenty-first-century Western church folk, discipleship is grounded in the calling to relationship with God through Jesus.

The First Vocation

The traditional formula for Christian catechism includes the question, "What is the chief end of man?" The response to that question is worded variously as "To glorify God and enjoy him forever!" (Westminster Shorter Catechism, 1647); "To know God by whom men were created" (Genevan Catechism, 1541); and "By the end of man we mean the purpose for which he was created, namely to know, love, and serve God" (Baltimore Catechism, 1891). These responses remind us of the primary vocation of human beings, which was damaged in the fall and redeemed by Jesus: to be in relationship with God.

In the summer following second grade, I had a consuming crush on a boy named Bruce. While I barely registered on the status meter of elementary-school social hierarchy, Bruce was quite popular, and try as I might, I could not get him to return my affections. On warm afternoons during the school break, I would hike down by the cool creek that ran beside our yard. I spent considerable time on these rambles thinking about Bruce. One day I picked a daisy that grew up between the rocks that bordered the creek bed and began plucking the petals, reciting, "He loves me. He loves me not." I convinced myself that if I ended on "He loves me," Bruce would magically return my ardor. And so I did. But he didn't. Plucking the final petal, I shivered with excitement, "He loves me!" and yet, his sentiments didn't change.

Magic cannot create relationship. In fact, magical thinking impedes relationship. Whenever we participate in activities designed to induce another to act, think, or feel a certain way, we are engaging in magic, precluding relationship by turning the other into an "it" rather than a "who." Yet it is surprising how easily magic creeps into Christianity. When I find myself feeling disillusioned about Sunday mornings, I often wonder when worship as celebration became "going to church" as an act of obedience that appeases God. If we approach worship, Bible reading, participation in rituals, financial donation, or other "religious activities" as attempts to win God's favor, they become magic, every bit as much as dancing around a fire chanting incantations on moonlit nights. If, on the other hand, we approach these practices as ways to spend time with God, then we are involved in relationship.

Relationships are powerful. I recall a friend who had been all "prickles and burrs" in seminary. His anger was notorious among the students, and his hostility frequently erupted in tirades against professors. He didn't just have anger—he was an angry person. I developed a friendship with this man when we worked on a project together. I learned that he had had a damaging upbringing and was coming out of a difficult end to an incompatible marriage. These relationships had left him in a perpetual state of defensiveness. I wondered at graduation time how he would fare in ministry or, more pointedly, how a church would fare in his hands. A decade later, I was leading a seminar for a regional meeting when I noticed my old angry friend among the participants. The face was familiar, but I saw differences beyond those made by the passage of years. At break time, I connected with my prickly friend. Only he wasn't prickly anymore. He radiated a gracious, gentle spirit and laughed easily, in a way that seemed to celebrate sheer joy in life. As we were speaking, some people joined us, and he introduced me to a small entourage from his church. These people obviously adored him. His final introduction was of a gentle-faced woman with whom he exchanged looks of obvious devotion. "This is my wife," he said, beaming. The cause of the difference was clear. This man's relationships with his church members and with his wife had created a safe place within which he could reclaim his inner kindness and joy. Relationships with others have the power to change us.

The power of human relationships offers a mere glimpse of the capacity of relationship with God in Jesus to transform us. Jesus promised us "an Advocate, the Spirit of truth," to use the Johannine terminology, who abides with us and in us (John 14:15–17). This indwelling Spirit makes possible a transformation of self that affects all of our other relationships. Our primary vocation to be in relationship with God, which was redeemed for us by Jesus, makes possible restoration, renewal, and reclamation of three other vocations; namely, the call to be human, to serve as a prophetic-symbolic presence, and to practice dominion.

The Restored Vocation of Being Fully Human

Primary among the relationships rejuvenated by our relationship with God through Jesus is the one we have with ourselves. In chapter 4, we noted that discipleship is an integrated way of being, one in which we are atoned—able to be at one with ourselves. This change of relationship with the self is not a matter of adopting some other identity but rather of recovering the authentic identity given us by our Creator and witnessed to by the Spirit, who testifies "that we are children of God" (Rom. 8:16).

As most of us know from experience, this oneness of self is neither a static state nor one fully achieved in earthly life. Unkind people, challenging circumstances, and habitual self-denigration all conspire to rob us of the relationship with ourselves made possible through God's grace. Again and again, we need the Spirit to remind us who we are and to empower us to grow toward what the second-generation Pauline communities called "the measure of the full stature of Christ" (Eph. 4:13).

The journey metaphor is an apt and popular way to frame our "in-process" condition. The image is not without its weaknesses, however. On the one hand, journey language can be used to excuse poor behavior and evade personal responsibility: "Well, I'm not perfect; I'm on a journey!" On the other hand, the concept can reflect a focus on the goal that interferes with our experience of the journey, reinforcing the very drivenness that characterizes our culture and runs contrary to discipleship.

One of the changes in contemporary life is the loss of enjoyment of road trips. In the "old days," driving could be a pleasurable activity, and children used to enjoy the scenery flicking past the window. Nowadays, driving is often a stressful venture, and children frequently submerge themselves in video games and DVDs, oblivious to the view, which is often of multilane highways packed with other cars with other stressed-out drivers and diverted children. The process of getting there used to be as much fun as the destination itself. Nowadays, travel is often just a matter of getting there as quickly and painlessly as possible. We drive to arrive. This change in the nature of travel may contaminate the journey metaphor, which once bespoke being present in the moment and valuing the process as much as the destination. Walking with Jesus can then become walking toward some notion of having arrived with an intensity that means missing Jesus on the way. We can be so focused on some not-yet-arrived-at destination—being super good, super spiritual, superhuman—that we miss the journey of being simply human in God's grace. The restored vocation of being human means being fully present, basking in God's total acceptance of us, at peace with our authentic identity as created, redeemed human beings—in every moment of the journey.

A Renewed Prophetic-Symbolic Vocation

As Jesus redeems our relationship with God and restores our relationship with ourselves, he transforms how we relate to others. The people of God have always been called to live out among themselves a unique society in which is manifested the will of God and through which God is made known to the world. As a prophetic reformer within Judaism, Jesus renewed this call in his proclamation of the kingdom. This then is the twofold vocation of prophetic-symbolic presence: to create community and to serve the world.

Community

When Simon, Andrew, John, and James responded to Jesus's call to follow him, the act of following meant leaving the communities that defined them and forming a new community, which corresponded to their new identity as students of Jesus. After Jesus's resurrection and ascension, discipleship meant transforming other gatherings into Christian communities. Synagogues and households evolved into assemblies dedicated to the continuing ministry and presence of Jesus.[4] As the gospel spread, discipleship often meant becoming part of existing Christian communities. Whether through formation,

---

KINGDOM OF GOD

While Jesus is unique in his use of "kingdom of God," he captures and expands the theocentric servant-community concept of the Old Testament. For example, God promises that Abraham will become a great nation through whom all people will be blessed (Gen. 22:15–18). Israel is called to be "a priestly kingdom and a holy nation" (Exod. 19:6) and is condemned by the prophets when the people of Israel fail in this vocation.[3]

---

transformation, or admission, discipleship presupposes participation in a community that is defined by and also reveals the presence of Jesus. Consider, as an illustration, the description of the church in Acts offered by former religious education professor Marianne Sawicki:

> The cooperative, mutually supportive spirit of the community is presented by the author of Acts as one of the signs and wonders that accompany the proclamation of the gospel. The forgiveness of sins seems to be experienced not so much as a future benefit between individuals and God, but as a present condition facilitating brotherly-sisterly care among the members of the community.[5]

The vocation of prophetic-symbolic presence propels us to create communities that anticipate the kingdom of God, that reveal in their common life the conquest of death through grace, and that in so doing bear witness to God's presence in the world. As we are called to relationships of "brotherly and sisterly care" with other disciples, living out the kingdom in our communities, we are also called to live the kingdom in our relationships with the world.

Service

All living beings are creations of God, and Christ died for all. This is the lens of grace given us through our relationship with Jesus. By our own experiences of grace, we are set free from coercion, manipulation, judgment, presumption, and the need to "fix" those around us. Our calling to prophetic-symbolic presence means serving others as divine creations for whom Jesus died. This call to continue Jesus's ministry, especially among those in need, is beautifully expressed in a prayer of the Spanish mystic Teresa of Avila:

> Christ has no body now on earth but yours;
> yours are the only hands through which he can do his work,
> yours are the only feet through which he can go about the world,
> yours are the only eyes through which his compassion can shine forth
> upon a troubled world
> Christ has no body now on earth but yours.[6]

TERESA OF AVILA

Born in 1515 into an aristocratic family, Teresa of Avila experienced two dramatic transformations in her life. During an illness as a teenager, her reading of Jerome's writings converted her interests from fashion and romance to a life dedicated to God. At age twenty, she joined a convent against her family's wishes. Two decades later, a vision led her to found a convent with a much stricter rule than that of the easygoing convents of her day. Her convent multiplied into the religious order known as the "barefoot" Carmelites.

The prophetic-symbolic vocation means being the hands, feet, voice, and very presence of Jesus in the world.

The discussion of the final judgment in Matthew reveals that service to others is not peripheral to discipleship.

> Then the king will say to those on his right, "My father blessed you! Come and receive the kingdom that was prepared for you before the world was created. When I was hungry, you gave me something to eat, and when I was thirsty, you gave me something to drink. When I was a stranger, you welcomed me and when I was naked, you gave me clothes to wear. When I was sick, you took care of me and when I was in jail, you visited me.
> . . . Whenever you did it for any of my people, no matter how unimportant they seemed, you did it for me."
> —MATTHEW 25:34–36, 40 CEV

Service to the unimportant is a central measure of the authenticity of discipleship. The word translated "unimportant," or more commonly "least," generally indicates smallest in size, last in rank, or least honorable. It suggests the smallest of the small and the least of the least, those with the lowest stature and most limited power in society.[7] The renewed vocation of prophetic symbolic presence calls us to be the presence of God by creating gracious communities and offering gracious service to those considered valueless by our society.

The Reclaimed Vocation of Dominion

As a sect within Judaism, early Christianity held to an understanding that in the ministry of Jesus a shift had taken place that affects all of the created order. This belief in the cosmic character of salvation was so important to first-generation communities that the mission of sharing the gospel beyond Judaism included introducing Gentile converts to the Jewish eschatological concepts that laid the foundation for this belief. If the fall did indeed affect all aspects of the created order, then the remedy—that is, Jesus—must necessarily also have an impact on the entire created order, a notion supported in Paul's exposition of the gospel:

> In fact, all creation is eagerly waiting for God to show who his children are. Meanwhile, creation is confused, but not because it wants to be confused. God made it this way in the hope that creation would be set free from decay and would share in the glorious freedom of his children.
>
> —ROMANS 8:19–21 CEV

The redeemed relationship with God through Jesus, therefore, affects not only our relationships with other believers and with the world, but also our relationship with the rest of creation.

Genesis 1:28b presents the Creator's directive to human beings to "fill the earth and subdue it, and have dominion over the fish of the sea, and over the birds of the air and over every living thing that moves upon the earth." The fact that humans have power within the created order is fairly obvious. What is often overlooked, however, is the crucial detail that since this power was conferred by the Creator, the Creator gets to define how we use it. In fact, immediately following the call to dominion, we see God placing limits on the use of that power:

> See, I have given you every plant yielding seed that is upon the face of all the earth, and every tree with seed in its fruit; you shall have them for food. And to every beast of the earth, and to every bird of the air, and to everything that creeps on the earth, everything that has the breath of life, I have given every green plant for food.
>
> —GENESIS 1:29–30

God defines what is available for food and makes it clear that humans do not get to use everything; some of the bounty of the earth is given for the other creatures with whom we share this habitat. Human dominion, then, is *relative* dominion. The exercise of our power within the created order is qualified by God's sovereignty over us. We are God's envoys, earthly representatives of the Creator, and when we live out dominion *in ways that reflect divine intent*, we bear witness to God's authority as Creator.

Other texts in Scripture shed light on divine intent and the parameters of our mandate. The second creation story, in Genesis 2:4b–3:24, speaks of God's placing the man in the Garden of Eden to "till it and keep it" (2:15), an image of caring for and preserving creation. The call to compassionate treatment of creation and other creatures is evidenced elsewhere in the Bible, especially in the legal material that was designed to guide Israel in living out God's will. Consider, for example, the institution of the sabbatical year:

> Six years you shall sow your field, and six years you shall prune your vineyard, and gather in their yield; but in the seventh year there shall be a sabbath of complete rest for the land, a sabbath for the Lord; you shall not sow your field or prune your vineyard. You shall not

---

CREATION, ANIMALS, AND DOMINION

The word in Genesis 1:28b that is translated as "subdue" does carry a sense of forcing into submission, which likely reflects the context of the ancestors of Israel. Nature was a powerful and dangerous force, much less within the understanding and control of people than it is today. The word translated as "dominion" is the Hebrew *rada*. The term has a broad range of meanings, from "tread" to "accompany." Protection for animals in the legal material includes the sabbatical year (Exod. 23:10 and Lev. 25:3–7); prohibitions against bestiality (Exod. 22:18; Lev. 20:15–16; Deut. 27:21); and directives for compassionate treatment in Deuteronomy: 22:1–4 (Exod. 23:4–5); 22:6–7; 22:10; and 25:4.[8]

reap the aftergrowth of your harvest or gather the grapes of your unpruned vine: it shall be a year of complete rest for the land. You may eat what the land yields during its sabbath—you, your male and female slaves, your hired and your bound laborers who live with you; for your livestock also, and for the wild animals in your land all its yield shall be for food.

—LEVITICUS 25:3–7 (ALSO EXOD. 23:10)

This period of rest reveals God's protection and care, not just for people but also for the land and its other-than-human creatures.

Instead of using the power given us by God to care for creation, humans have consistently chosen to treat creation in selfish, short-sighted, and destructive ways, using it in complete disregard for the limits set by God. The ultimate model for use of power, of course, is Jesus, who lovingly and sacrificially used his power on behalf of the entire created order. This is the model for a reclaimed vocation of dominion: to experience through relationship with Jesus the trans-formation of our relationships within the created order into the lov-ing relative sovereignty that exemplifies Jesus's lordship over all—a vocation described in "The Rime of the Ancient Mariner."

And to teach, by his own example,
Love and reverence
To all things that God made and loveth.

Farewell, farewell! but this I tell
To thee, thou Wedding-Guest!
He prayeth well, who loveth well
Both man and bird and beast.

He prayeth best, who loveth best
All things both great and small;
For the dear God who loveth us,
He made and loveth all.
—SAMUEL TAYLOR COLERIDGE [9]

Discipleship is grounded in the primary vocation of redeemed relationship with God through Jesus. By transforming us, the relationship with God issues forth changes in all other relationships, namely in the restored, renewed, and reclaimed vocations of being human, of prophetic-symbolic presence, and of dominion. If discipleship is grounded in vocation, then a foundational question for discipleship formation is this: How do we teach vocation?

Teaching Vocation, Nurturing Relationship

Education is an invitational endeavor. We cannot compel, manipulate, or otherwise coerce people to enter into relationship with any subject matter. Vocational education rests on three interrelated pillars: theoretical foundation, experience, and apprenticeship.

Theoretical Foundation: Christian Tradition

The theoretical foundation of discipleship is the Christian tradition, complete with its Jewish roots. It is the story we find in the Scriptures, both Old and New Testament, and find encapsulated in Christian hymnody, creedal formulations, and communal rituals. To form disciples we must tell the story, but before telling it, we must know the story.

On one of my home visits to an elderly "saint" of the church, she began her usual practice of telling stories about her home health-care provider. The woman explained that her provider was not as clean as she should be, and so one day, she gave her a lecture on cleanliness, closing with "and, as the Bible says, 'Cleanliness is next to godliness.'" While the cleanliness adage might be a valuable one, it does not come from the Bible. The axiom, which was quoted by John Wesley, is attested to in the writings of Francis Bacon in 1605 and may have been drawn from a second-century Hebrew proverb. Over the years, I have compiled a fairly long list of popular adages that are frequently "quoted" from the Bible, none of which are actually biblical material. I recently heard a popular quote in a favorite detective show.

In this episode, a rabbi explained to detectives that the directive to "spare the rod and spoil the child" is frequently misused because it is taken out of its context in the Bible. The rabbi was correct in suggesting that the saying is taken out of context but incorrect in identifying that context as biblical. The quotation is not from the Bible, but from a seventeenth-century burlesque poem, *Hudibras*, and refers to quelling "romantic" feelings.[10] In a later episode of the same program, a lawyer cross-examining a minister referred to Mary Magdalene as a prostitute. The minister responded by explaining that Jesus had forgiven Mary, and she had changed her ways. It's a shame that the script editors didn't check the reference to Mary Magdalene. If they had, they would have discovered that she was not a prostitute but a woman of means, a disciple of Jesus, and one of the first to witness and proclaim his resurrection.[11] Unfortunately, the errant image of Mary as an adulterous prostitute, which was introduced early in church history and has permeated our culture through decades of "Jesus movies," was further perpetuated in this television program.

These instances draw attention to two threats to our providing theoretical foundations for discipleship: biblical illiteracy among Christians and the hijacking of our tradition by the culture. Both trends result in propagation of ignorance and misuse of the tradition. It is more important than ever that we know and share our tradition. Our visit with the earliest Christian communities revealed that the risen Christ is actually present in the telling of the Christian story. It is essential that we tell the story—not talk about the story, not give directives based on the story, not modify or abridge the story—but tell the story. We need to tell the story with our words, through our relationships, and in our actions and to trust its power as a vehicle of Christ's presence.

Experience: Encounter with God

As relationship with God is the primary vocation of discipleship, the principal experience for discipleship formation is encounter with God through Jesus. When I was a pastor, I was blessed to serve in a community that had a remarkable ecumenical ethos. Through our council of churches, the American Baptists, Presbyterians, United Methodists, Roman Catholics, and Wesleyans all worked together to offer a variety of activities to the community. One summer night we gathered in the

Presbyterian fellowship hall for an evangelistic event for older children and teens. The evening began with a group of bodybuilders giving testimonies and continued with the guests breaking up into discussion groups. Since I wasn't assigned to a group, I spent my time helping with snacks and visiting rooms to see if anyone needed anything. As I approached one doorway, I heard a young women pleading, "Even if you don't believe it's true, just do me a favor and say the prayer with me. If it's not true, you haven't lost anything. It if turns out to be true, then you'll be saved, and when you die, you will go to heaven." This was the first time, but not the last, that I heard this shocking approach to "evangelism."

Reducing Christianity to a matter of final destination is manipulative, of course, but this approach also suggests that how we live out the faith in our earthly lives is of secondary importance. Most readers would likely agree that the practice of repeating particular words, irrespective of belief and regardless of desire for relationship with God, as a guarantee of going to heaven is pure magic. The question for those of us who reject this and other magical approaches is, what do we do instead? How do we encourage and nurture the primary vocation of discipleship, which is relationship with God through Jesus? The enterprise is complicated by the fact that Jesus is not physically present, at least not in the ways that we typically understand physical presence. We need to identify, therefore, the ways in which Jesus is present and invite people to an encounter with Jesus through those venues.

Although they described the experience in a variety of ways, the earliest Christian communities were formed around the very presence of Jesus. Jesus was present through his Spirit, who gave believers the power, discernment, and skills necessary to live out Christian community. He was present in the gathered community as master teacher and guide. His presence was evidenced in the love that members shared with one another, in the ongoing ministry of his followers to the world, and in the traditions that were taught as the gospel was proclaimed. The earliest communities of Jesus followers, then, suggest two additional venues for encountering God by experiencing the presence of Jesus: community and service, two avenues of apprenticeship in the vocations of discipleship.

Apprenticeship: Participation and Practice

In the discussion found in Matthew 18 about settling disputes, Jesus advises, "For where two or three are gathered in my name, I am there among them" (v. 20). When speaking about relationships among church members, Paul calls the community "the body of Christ," a sentiment that is developed in the second generation's vision of the idealized church (Col. 2:19; Eph. 5:23). The Johannine community bears witness to the Spirit of Jesus, who abides with believers as advocate and teacher and who generates love within the community (John 14:15–15:17; 1 John 3:11–24). Although they frame the experience in a variety of ways, each of the communities evidences dependence on the tangible presence of the risen Christ. As we live out discipleship and seek to nurture discipleship in others, we assume responsibility for forming communities that manifest the presence of Jesus, communities that are so dependent on and influenced by Jesus that he is made known through participation in the gathered body of disciples.

If we revisit the description of the final judgment in Matthew 25:31–46, we can see that service is inherent in discipleship, not only because of Jesus's admonition but also because of Jesus's presence. In the act of service, we encounter Jesus: "Whenever you did it for any of my people, no matter how unimportant they seemed, you did it for me"; and "Whenever you failed to help any of my people, no matter how unimportant they seemed, you failed to do it for me" (Matt. 25:40, 45 CEV). Jesus identifies with "the least" and is present with them. The call to care for the powerless and marginalized provides the ultimate opportunity for service-learning projects, not merely to learn and teach "Christian charity" but also to grow in relationship with Jesus. As we become the presence of Jesus in ministry to others, we also experience the presence of Jesus in those we seek to serve. To care for the unimportant is to encounter Jesus. The gracious irony is that as we seek to bring Jesus to those who live defenseless on the periphery of society, we find him already there, waiting for us.

We can see how intertwined the three pillars of vocational education are when we speak of the vocations of discipleship, which are relational in nature. As we practice one aspect of vocational education, such as theoretical foundation, we also practice another— for example, experience. Teaching the tradition makes Jesus present and provides opportunity for encounter with him. At this point, readers may also have noted the interdependence of the vocations: the relationship with Jesus transforms all of our relationships; the practice of transformed relationships then also nurtures the relationship with Jesus, which continues to transform our other relationships—and on it goes. This interdependence reveals the dynamic nature of discipleship. We were created for relationship with God, we become disciples through Jesus, and we continue to evolve in discipleship through the practices of transformed relationships.

I recently viewed a 1976 documentary about James Alfred Wight, better known as James Herriot, author of *All Creatures Great and Small* and other books about his work as a Yorkshire veterinarian.[12] In the interview, Herriot described his struggle to become the writer we see at work in his books. He had been an avid reader throughout his life and had developed into a skilled essayist through his schooling. He also had a natural gift for writing, yet his work was repeatedly turned down by publishers. When asked how he learned to write in the style that made his books so popular, he answered, "I practiced. I kept writing and writing." Even as a natural writer, James Herriot found it necessary to develop his profound relationship with the written word, to nurture the writer within through practice of the vocation of writing. Herriot's experience in writing provides an apt metaphor for discipleship. We are disciples. We are in relationship to God through Jesus. Yet, to become fully the disciples we are designed to be, we need to practice the vocations of discipleship through which we develop intimacy with God and move toward "the measure of the full stature of Christ."

Exercises for Individuals or Groups

1. As a devotional activity, select a favorite story from the Gospels and arrange a time to hear it anew. Gather your Bible, a hymnbook, or perhaps a CD of favorite hymns. Hear the story by reading it and listening to a hymn that relates to the story. Spend some time reliving the story, imagining the details, the sights, sounds, smells, and emotions of the story. Enter into silence, and allow the story to touch you with

the presence of Jesus. If you are part of a group, engage in this activity privately; then discuss ways in which you might invite others to experience Jesus through the story.

2. The vocation of service compels us to look honestly at our culture and ask, "Who are the least?" Those identified in Matthew—the alien, the poor, the ill and imprisoned—are still among us. Are there others who stand at the margins of our culture or even of our churches? Alone or working with a group, specify those who are "unimportant" and ways in which you might offer apprenticeships in the vocation of service.

6

Nurtured within Community

By the images of the group's special language, the poetic reiteration of statements and metaphors of fundamental beliefs, reinforced by musical rhythms, charged with the high emotional level induced by cumulative interaction in the meetings, the group's peculiar "knowledge" grows. With it, attitudes and dispositions take form; the kinds of behavior "worthy of the way you received Christ" are learned.

—WAYNE MEEKS, THE FIRST URBAN CHRISTIANS[1]

The Christian community nurtures Christian identity through all aspects of its life. We form disciples through education and enculturation, two interdependent and interwoven aspects of community life. In *To Set One's Heart*, Sara Little distinguishes teaching from socialization by its intentionality and focus on subject matter: "Teaching is used here to refer to those planned occasions in which designated teachers set up a process and structure for dealing with subject matter in such a way as to enable students to assess the truth of the same in terms of their own frame of reference."[2] Little's definition is broader than the one we considered in chapter 4 and can be considered a component of education, which I defined there as "a supportive endeavor that assists in bringing about new life." For the Christian community, teaching includes instruction and deliberately structured experiences that encourage encounter with God, personal development, and relationship building. Enculturation or socialization refers to becoming part of a given culture through participation, adopting its norms, attitudes, values, motives, social roles, language, and symbols. Participation in community life is a powerful force that can enhance or derail our teaching efforts. Authentic Christian discipleship can be nurtured only within authentic Christian community; therefore, in this chapter we will survey five marks of authentic Christian community and five practices that help us create such communities.

CURRICULUM AND SOCIALIZATION

While we often use *curriculum* in reference to printed instructional materials, the word has a much broader meaning, which includes both what we intend to teach and what we inadvertently teach. The power of socialization to form identity demands that we attend to the entire range of curricula that are at work in the community of faith.

- *Explicit or intended curriculum* refers to what is presented as part of an intentional educational agenda. Explicit curriculum in the faith community includes Sunday school plans, Bible texts, creeds, descriptions of rituals, and membership requirements.
- *Implicit, hidden, or covert curriculum* refers to what is learned by the nature of a group. Hidden curriculum in the faith community is found in its structure and routines and in the behaviors, attitudes, and relationships of its members.
- *Null curriculum* consists of what we choose not to teach. In faith communities, the null curriculum might include books of the Bible or individual texts that we choose not to study or topics that we avoid.
- *Concomitant curriculum* refers to what is taught or emphasized at home, outside the primary educational site. Venues for concomitant curriculum of the faith community also include denominational and ecumenical life.
- *Received or learned curriculum* refers to those things that participants take from the experience. Received curriculum provides the measure of effectiveness for our discipleship enterprise, because it reflects the actual results of our efforts.

Before we begin our explorations, we need to note an important distinguishing characteristic of first-century personality as noted by theology professor Bruce J. Malina (Creighton University) and New Testament professor Jerome H. Neyrey (Notre Dame):

> Our hypothesis is that first-century Mediterranean persons were strongly group-embedded, collectivist persons. Since they were group-oriented, they were "socially" minded, as opposed to "psychologically" minded. They were attuned to the values, attitudes, and beliefs of their in-group, with which they shared a common fate due to generation and geography. Thanks to their in-group enculturation, they were used to assessing themselves and others in terms of stereotypes often explained as deriving from family "history" and the geographical location of their group.[3]

The authors' description of the first-century personality as communally defined can help us understand the New Testament practice of identifying people by their households (Rom. 10:10; 2 Tim. 4:19) and the phenomenon of entire households being baptized (Acts 16:15; 1 Cor. 1:16). It also helps us appreciate the use of "family" or "household" as an image of the church, for example:

> So then, you are no longer strangers and aliens, but you are citizens with the saints and also members of the household of God, built upon the foundations of the apostles and prophets, with Christ Jesus himself as the cornerstone.
>
> —Ephesians 2:19–20

In a culture in which the identity of individuals was defined by family, designating the community of faith as a "family" (Gal. 5:22) or "household" underscored the fact that becoming a follower of Jesus meant making a dramatic change in self-understanding; a change in which one's very identity is formed no longer by the family of origin but by the family of faith.

The significance of the communal self-understanding of the earliest Christians for our discussion lies in the contrast between their mind-set and that of contemporary Westerners. Because we live in an individualistic culture, the communal identity that was a given in the first century is not necessarily part of our self-understanding. Although we inherently understand the personal accountability that is part of discipleship, we sometimes emphasize individual responsibility to the point of overlooking the communal character of the faith and then underappreciate the power of community to form disciples. This tendency means that we need to attend consciously to the role of Christian community in Christian education. That is, we need to recognize that since socialization is a powerful force in the formation of identity, the *nature* of our communities is of utmost importance. True discipleship is formed in true Christian community. Therefore, the success of any community in contributing to the formation of followers of Jesus directly correlates to its authenticity. We need to ask the question, "What constitutes *authentic* Christian community?"

The Marks of Authentic Christian Community

An authentic Christian community is one that practices the presence of Jesus. I've chosen *practice* deliberately here, because the word points toward the reality that true Christian community both experiences the presence of Jesus in its midst and embodies the presence of Jesus for the world. Authentic Christian community is, therefore, *radical* community, a term that need not frighten us. The primary meaning of *radical* is "arising from or going to a root or source."[4] True Christian communities are utterly dependent on Jesus as their root—the source and sustenance of the community. As our source and sustenance, Jesus creates a distinct way of being within the community, which in itself helps to form Christian identity. This distinctiveness isn't about being different for difference's sake, however. While *different* can imply defining ourselves in contrast to something outside ourselves (we are different *from* other groups), Christian distinctiveness is a positive concept. It implies defining ourselves *by* something—or better, *by someone*, namely Jesus.

As we saw in section 1, the primitive Christian communities, while sharing marks of authenticity, were striking in their diversity. For example, the egalitarian hopes of the entirely Jewish Jerusalem community led to the development of a Christian collective that practiced communal sharing of resources. This manifestation of Christian community was a response to the poverty experienced by many of its members. By comparison, the Pauline communities, whose membership was drawn from the highly stratified larger society, were focused on how to be one in Christ. The status issues that came from their context required emphasis on freedom (there were slaves and slaveholders in the communities), on the Spirit (who gifts all believers), and on the body of Christ (which needs all those gifted members). The very fact that Christian communities differed from one another is testament to their authenticity, because their differences demonstrate responsiveness to their particular settings. Responsiveness is one distinguishing mark of authentic Christian community.

Responsiveness

Responsiveness to changing external contexts and internal circumstances was essential to the continuation and spread of the gospel. According to Marianne Sawicki, the ability to change is one of the most conventional aspects of our Christian heritage:

> The most traditional thing about the [early] Christian churches is their adaptability, their readiness to change to accommodate new needs in new times, while preserving—more or less faithfully to be sure!—their continuity with the message and work of Jesus Christ.[5]

It is important not to miss the irony here. Christian community rests on ancient tradition, which we might be inclined to preserve by insulating ourselves from change. Yet the ability to be untraditional is essential to that very tradition, because adaptability makes possible preservation of the tradition for each new age and context.

Internal circumstances and external context are not the only realities to which Christian community is responsive, though. Jesus, as our source, power, authority, and primary teacher, continually guides the community, making Christian community not only a teaching community, but also a perpetually learning community. The fact that we are continuously learning is in itself educational, demonstrating that to follow Jesus is to walk a path of growth and change in response to Jesus. This dependence on Jesus for our existence and survival engenders within the community an attitude of thankfulness. A second mark of authentic Christian community, then, is gratitude.

Gratitude

For Valentine's Day one year, I did a children's sermon in which I gave each of the children a flower as a reminder of God's love for them. With wide-eyed smiles, they proudly and carefully carried their little treasures back to their pews. Later, as Sunday school began, one of the adults arrived huffing, "I am so ashamed. Not one of those children said 'thank you.'" She was late for the adult class, because she had taken time to admonish the children for their oversight. After class, one by one, remorseful children shuffled their way to me to apologize and say, "Thank you for the flower." No happy saunters. No smiling eyes. My respond to each child was, "I appreciate your words, but I already heard you say thank you. I heard it in your smile and in the way you handled your flower." The children may not have expressed their gratitude in the "right" way, but genuine thankfulness had emanated from them. The children's gratitude had issued from their belief that I had given them flowers simply to show them love—no conditions, no expectations. Once the "should" entered the equation, the authenticity of their celebration was replaced with perfunctory words.

Christian community deals not in obligatory politeness and pretense but in the currency of real gratitude. Gratitude is an earthy, irrepressible, lived response to the love of God freely offered through Jesus. Gratitude flows from experienced need and received grace. Grace is a third mark of authentic Christian community.

Grace

One year special invitations were sent to our church's inactive list for our Christmas Eve events. The only people who accepted were a couple who stopped by the reception following worship on their way to the country club. Casting a nostalgic eye around, the woman commented, "We had such fun in youth group. Do the kids still come today?" When

I explained that the active membership had dwindled to twenty-five "over-sixties," she sighed, "That's such a shame. We had a great youth group." She spent some time that evening reminiscing with church members and recalling other former youth-group members, most of whom were also not active in any church. All agreed that those were great times, that it was a shame the church was failing, and that it was too bad parents didn't bring their children anymore. I wondered to myself why this "great" youth group hadn't succeeded in forming lifelong disciples of Jesus.

Both our Old and New Testaments testify to grace as God's attitude toward us, which is revealed in historic loving actions. In Christian understanding, grace is most clearly expressed in Jesus. Grace was also actualized in the early churches, as they shared the gospel (Acts 11:23), as their leaders continued despite personal weakness (Rom. 5:8, 16:20), and in their common interactions (such as gracious speech, Col. 4:6) and uncommon ones (for example, the collection taken by the other communities for the poor in Jerusalem, 2 Cor. 8). From start to finish, discipleship depends on God's grace. Our visitor was obviously sentimental about her youth-group experiences, but sentimentality is not gratitude, and fond memories are not grace. Good times can be offered by any number of social organizations. It is the distinct task of the church to provide a place where people encounter grace and see grace at work making possible the impossible—communion with God and one another. Communion is a fourth mark of authentic Christian community.

Communion

The call of Paul's letter to the Galatians for Christians to "work for the good of all, and especially for those of the family of faith" (6:10) is preceded by a description of the unique quality of community life made possible through the Spirit: "By contrast, the fruit of the Spirit is love, joy, peace, patience, kindness, generosity, faithfulness, gentleness, and self-control" (Gal. 5:22). *Communion* or *fellowship* in the New Testament means to share in, to have in common, or to participate in.[6] Paul also uses *communion* to refer to the Lord's Supper (1 Cor. 10:16), which reveals our dependence on Jesus for our communion with one another. It is our shared communion with Christ that creates our fellowship with one another.

Several years ago, a report heralded an agreement between two denominations to "return to communion," meaning that they would now be able share the Lord's Supper together. The two groups had split decades earlier from within the same tradition over a variety of beliefs and practices. Division among Christians is common, and it misses the point that our shared relationship with Jesus is much more important than any of the details that divide us. The parameters for understanding Jesus's identity and ministry in the first century seem to have been quite broad. The early communities expressed their shared belief in Jesus in profoundly different ways, yet in Acts and in many of the letters of the New Testament, we see communities working hard to stay in communion. While some focused on Jesus's humanity and others on his divinity, a break in communion came only when there was a break in what Dunn refers to as the "bedrock" of the faith, which he defines as "the unity between the earthly Jesus and the exalted one who is somehow involved in or part of our encounter with God in the here and now."[7] When some members denied that Jesus had come in the flesh (a belief that they used to justify self-centered, self-indulgent lifestyles [2 Pet. 3; 1 John 2:18–3:18]), they created a break between the earthly Jesus and the exalted one and also caused a break in fellowship with other Christians.[8] If our Gospels are any indication, the diverse understandings of Jesus evident in the early Christian communities were actually necessary to provide future generations with a more complete witness of Jesus. Witness is a fifth mark of authentic Christian community.

Witness

Historically, Christian groups have gone in one of two directions in relationship to the world. Some have opted to withdraw from the world, while others have embedded themselves to the point of becoming part of, and even indebted to, the larger culture. The role of the Christian community to be *in* the world, but not *of* (or conformed to) the world (John 17:11, 14; Rom. 12:2) is a difficult one to get a handle on—unless we focus on our mission *to* the world. It is our purpose that gives form to the Christian community. As Sara Little describes it:

For every group, every institution, every action, when there has been a clear sense of purpose, a consciousness of mission, the life, belief, attitudes all seem to cohere.[9]

Inherent in the call to be a Christian community is the role of continuing a prophetic-symbolic presence through which the kingdom is made known in the world. Consider, for example, Peter and John's encounter with a lame man as they went up to the temple for prayer:

> The man saw Peter and John entering the temple, and he asked them for money. . . . But Peter said, "I don't have any silver or gold! But I will give you what I do have. In the name of Jesus Christ from Nazareth, get up and start walking." Peter then took him by the right hand and helped him up.
>
> At once the man's feet and ankles became strong, and he jumped up and started walking around and praising God.
>
> —ACTS 3:3, 6–8 CEV

The healing of the man led to a gathering of astonished people to whom Peter preached the gospel (Acts 3:11–26). Following the example of Jesus, these earliest church leaders revealed the kingdom through proclamation and action, the two prongs of witness to the world.

Effective formation of disciples depends largely on the Christian community's capacity to communicate, clearly and with integrity, the presence of Jesus in its internal life and in its relationships with the world. I have identified responsiveness, gratitude, grace, communion, and witness as marks of authentic Christian community. No doubt readers will be able to identify others. These marks serve as indicators of our potential to nurture committed disciples. Only if we acknowledge that our communities do not always successfully practice the presence of Jesus will we be able to turn to the work of becoming effective learners and teachers of discipleship. Being an authentic Christian community doesn't happen by magic, and it doesn't happen once for all time, so we turn now to the question: "How do we become authentic Christian communities?" Five practices, apparent in the earliest Christian communities, can help us experience and embody the presence of Jesus.

Celebrate

Worship framed the life of the first-generation Christian communities. They gathered at the temple, in synagogues, and in private homes to celebrate with formal prayer, fellowship meals, recitation of confessions, hymn singing, and rituals. The earliest Christians followed the practices of Judaism, of which they were a sect, with Sabbath worship, daily worship built around recited prayers, and annual festivals. As the gospel spread, Jesus followers continued to follow the model of daily, weekly, and annual celebration.[10]

When later generations saw a growing complexity of structure in church life, the Johannine community turned to the Spirit, reminding us that structures are less important than the spirit in which we worship:

> Believe me, the time is coming when you won't worship the Father either on this mountain or in Jerusalem. . . . But a time is coming, and it is already here! Even now the true worshipers are being led by the Spirit to worship the Father according to the truth.
>
> —JOHN 4:21–24 CEV

Early Christian worship had one focus: celebration of what God had done in Jesus. By contrast, we ask our weekly services to accomplish so many things that it can be difficult really to celebrate during that hour. Gathering for worship frequently begins with the *business* of announcements. Worship often serves as the only *instructional time* for pastors, and attendance is commonly framed as an *act of obedience* for the worshipers, many of whom limit their involvement to that one hour. Worship services are also regularly seen as a *tool for church growth*. Services are often planned not according to the needs of those present but according to the imagined needs of those we want to attract. This practice may miss the mark for both groups. For example, while I enjoy contemporary services, an experience I had in 2001 opened my eyes to how different my tastes are from those of the younger adults whom many churches hope to attract.

I was over forty and living in an apartment complex that housed mostly college students and young families. One Saturday, while I lounged by the pool, I found myself annoyed by the music blaring over the loudspeaker. "Gosh, I'm such an old fogy," I thought. I felt relieved when the twenty-something woman next to me exclaimed, "What's with this music!" I smiled to her in agreement, and she continued, "What do they think it is anyway—the *nineties*?" My "fogy meter" shot up past old fogy to *really* old fogy. Popular music changes rapidly. Many of the songs that flash across PowerPoint screens in "contemporary" worship services were written ten, twenty, or even thirty years ago and will feel old and outdated to most young adults, especially to unchurched young adults. More important, though, the "contemporary" music of churches often seems to interfere with the worship experience of many people who *are* present. On numerous occasions, I have watched worship-team members having a grand time while many of the worshipers struggle to sing unfamiliar words to syncopated rhythms. Designing services to attract new members can supersede the purpose of worship, which remains, as it was in the first century, to celebrate what God has done in Jesus.

Celebration is necessarily expressed in ways that have meaning for those celebrating. Since the people who follow Jesus are diverse, real worship will vary dramatically among and even within churches. Worship is not generic celebration, however. It is celebration of our relationship with God. This means that true worship reflects the honestly held beliefs and experience of community members. If we worship as we think we should rather than in ways that have meaning for us, or if we celebrate what we don't actually believe, we may inadvertently teach that pretense is what is important, that saying the right words matters more to God than what is in our hearts. On the other hand, if we work together to create celebrations that match our natural (and varied) celebratory instincts and make sure that the hymns we sing, the prayers we say, the rituals we share, and the creeds we recite reflect our true beliefs, we demonstrate integrity and authenticity. That sort of communal effort requires love for one another.

Love

Love, according to the community of the Beloved Disciple, flows from God: "Beloved, let us love one another, because love is from God;

everyone who loves is born of God and knows God" (1 John 4:7). The Corinthian community provides a concrete definition of love that reflects its efforts to create a family of God out of a profoundly diverse membership:

> Love is patient; love is kind; love is not envious or boastful or arrogant or rude. It does not insist on its own way; it is not irritable or resentful; it does not rejoice in wrongdoing, but rejoices in the truth. It bears all things, believes all things, hopes all things, endures all things.
>
> —1 CORINTHIANS 13:4–7

Love is not about how we feel but about how we treat one another, and it can be manifested in the simplest of actions.

One Sunday morning a boy of about twelve came into our church a few minutes before worship began. The child was not from our neighborhood, although we'd occasionally seen him playing with children around the block. He came alone, dressed in a T-shirt and shorts, and a little sweaty from the summer's heat. At the door of the sanctuary, one of the church members discreetly slipped a dollar into his hand, so he wouldn't feel awkward at offering time. This scene repeated itself several times, and by the time the child made his way to a pew, he had a fistful of bills. These seemingly small acts were acts of love, because the people had put themselves in the boy's place and had taken action to protect him from discomfort.

As we strive to incarnate God's love in the interior life of the church, we need to realize that loving as Jesus loves doesn't necessarily mean being nice, as demonstrated in Jesus's response to a wealthy young man who asked him how to inherit eternal life.

> Jesus said to him, "Why do you call me good? No one is good but God alone. You know the commandments: 'You shall not murder; You shall not commit adultery; You shall not steal; You shall not bear false witness; You shall not defraud; Honor your father and mother.'" He said to him, "Teacher, I have kept all these since I my youth." Jesus, looking at him, loved him and said, "You lack one thing; go, sell what you own, and give the money to the poor, and you will have treasure

in heaven; then come, follow me." When he heard this, he was shocked and went away grieving, for he had many possessions.

—Mark 10:18–22 (ALSO FOUND IN MATT. 19:13–15 AND LUKE 18:18–30)

The text describes the man as "shocked" and "grieving," indicators that he probably did not think Jesus was being nice, but the story says that Jesus loved him. God's love for all people means having standards that protect the least among us. Those who care only for their own needs and desires may very well experience this type of love as "not nice." Because they are small in size and stature, children are significantly at risk in our world, so how we treat children is one very good gauge of whether we are practicing love.

The Gospel stories of Jesus welcoming children and proclaiming their importance clue us in to the earliest Jesus followers' attitude toward children.[11] In her analysis of children in the New Testament, Judith Gundry-Volf, senior research scholar at Yale Divinity School, concludes that the Christian Scriptures teach a view of children that is in such contrast to the dominant view that it requires changing "not only how adults relate to children but how we conceive our social world":

> Children are not only subordinate but sharers with adults in the life of faith; they are not only to be formed but to be imitated; they are not only ignorant but capable of receiving spiritual insight; they are not "just" children but representatives of Christ. . . . Jesus did not teach how to make an adult world kinder and more just for children; he taught the arrival of a social world in part defined by and organized around children.[12]

Sadly, this profound view of children is not always evidenced in Christian communities. We tend to push children to the side of church life, while at the same time holding them to standards of behavior for which they do not have the physical, emotional, or social maturity.[13] Consider, for example, the common assertion that making children sit quiet and still (something few adults do) in adult-sized pews through adult-designed and adult-led worship services somehow "teaches them respect." It more likely teaches them that, as my nephew once pointed out, "Church is boring!" We must rethink the place of children in the church, not because they are "our future" (how arrogant—and telling—that we frame children's value according to our own needs!), but because we create their present, a present in which we must share with them Jesus's love lest we become stumbling blocks to their faith. It would be better for us to have great millstones hung around our necks and be thrown into the sea (Matt. 18:6; Mark 9:42; and Luke 17:1–3).

The love practiced in the Christian community is not intended to remain within our walls. God's love for us is also the love God has for the world. It necessarily spills over in the form of service to others.

Serve

Earlier we noted that the encounter of Peter and John with the lame man allowed them to share the gospel through words and action. The significance of that event, however, went beyond the physical healing of a single man. By his infirmity, the man had been relegated to the fringes of society, where he was left utterly dependent on others for his survival. Some would have blamed the man's plight on sinfulness, and his malady rendered him unclean and untouchable. Peter and John invited the man to meet their gaze—a sign of equality (Acts 3:4). Risking becoming unclean himself, Peter reached out to the man with his *right* hand—the hand of strength and power—through which flowed a healing. Peter and John altered the man's status in society and challenged the social structures of the day.[14] This prophetic-symbolic act revealed the nature of God's kingdom as a realm in which oppressive human structures are broken down and in which those deemed unacceptable by people are welcomed by God. It amazed the crowds (Acts 3:11) and scared the leaders of the status quo to the point that they jailed the pair (Acts 4:1–3), much as they had jailed their master, who had sacrificed himself to bring good news to the poor (Luke 4:18).

A few years ago, I received a call from the funeral director in a town I'd left nearly two decades earlier. A parishioner of the church I'd served there had died, and since the church was between pastors, he asked if I could return to preside over the funeral already scheduled for the following Wednesday. I explained that although I'd like to oblige, it would be difficult to take vacation time on such short notice, and my budget wouldn't allow me to cover the expense of the 450-mile round trip. He was a bit annoyed and said he'd find someone else. He then began to lament the condition of the churches in the area, suggesting that their decline was due to today's ministers not caring for their flocks, by which he meant not doing sufficient visitation and one-on-one caretaking. Somewhere along the line, Christian churches went from being communities of service to communities of "serve-us." Our mission to celebrate and share the presence of Jesus in the world is our *raison d'être*. Without it, we needn't exist. The failure of many of our churches, I suspect, began long ago when they lost any sense of themselves as communities of mutual service to one another and mission to the world.

As a pastor, I repeatedly heard church members refer to difficult situations and say, "The church really should do something." That statement betrayed a lack of understanding that they themselves were the church that they believed needed to do something. Ironically, our preoccupation with survival has often left us not only without any mission to the world, but also in a position of expecting the world to meet our needs. We rail against challenges to our status in the culture and demand legislation that protects our privileged place of the past. We rely on fundraisers through which the community is invited to help replace our roofs and repair our organs, and we frequently utter the bizarre plea, "Our church needs young families if it is going to survive," which suggests that it is the job of others to help the church rather than the job of the church, as in its members, to serve others. Our fear of demise burdens us to the point that there is little chance for love to grow in our midst, let alone to spill out to the world. If we do reach out, the people Jesus served—the sick, the imprisoned, the sinful, the ostracized, and the hungry—are not likely the ones we want to find at the end of our reach. After all, what can they bring to our church to help it survive? Yet only when we can free ourselves from our fears and prejudices to reach out boldly as did Peter, John, and countless other disciples of the first century will we know the power of Jesus's presence in new life-and-world-changing ways. To do that, we need to lighten our load.

Travel Light

When Jesus sent his apostles out into the world, he told them to travel light:

> He ordered them to take nothing for their journey except a staff;
> no bread, no bag, no money in their belts; but to wear sandals and
> not to put on two tunics.
>
> —MARK 6:8–9

Traveling light is essential to fulfilling our call to bring the gospel to the world, but as the Christian church became focused early in the fourth century on power and property—things that the world esteems—we lost sight of the kingdom whose values run counter to the values of the world.[15] We've become encumbered with status, buildings, activities, and complex dogma that can get in the way of our love for one another and our mission to the world. We need to shed some baggage.

Shedding baggage means freeing ourselves from buildings that take from us but no longer help us fulfill our role of prophetic symbolic presence. Perhaps freeing ourselves means not getting rid of property but rethinking the use of property in light of Jesus's call to care for the least. How many churches sit warm and empty while people shiver in homelessness? How many well-applianced church kitchens are unused between fundraising dinners while children's bellies are empty?

A church I once served housed a community Christian preschool that had a scholarship program for needy children. Throughout my time there, I experienced an ongoing battle to keep the church's commitment (made before my time) to provide space for the school, which met in the rarely used basement. The bathrooms were on the main floor, so the children had to gather upstairs for a daily break. The children had hands, and the church had painted walls—a perfect recipe for the handprints that infuriated one church member. Another was grieved by the occasional clogged toilet, and others saw as a deal breaker the once-a-year conflict between the preschool and the new-to-you sale, which apparently could not be set up in any of the church's other empty spaces. These members didn't respond well

THE SUNDAY SCHOOL MOVEMENT

The present-day Sunday school is a faint echo of the movement begun in England in the 1780s by Robert Raikes, Thomas Stock, and William Fox to meet the educational needs of children who had migrated to cities to work in factories. Newspaper owner and prison reformer Raikes came to associate the increase in prison population with a lack of education, so he turned his attention to educating the lower classes on Sundays, efforts that also kept unsupervised children off the streets on their one day off from work. By 1785 Sunday school claimed 65,000 participants in England, a success not appreciated by everyone. In general, the upper class opposed educating the poor, and church leaders resisted Sunday school's association with reform movements, its violation of Sunday as a day of rest, and its focus on secular subjects.

Within a decade, Sunday school had made its way to the United States where, following the British design, it used paid teachers and the Bible to provide rudimentary instruction that would help child workers become good citizens of the new republic. The Sunday school movement was both a critique and a product of its culture. At its best, Sunday school stood against the culture in insisting on basic education for all. At its worst, it was blind to injustice and promoted a nationalistic agenda and moralistic intolerance. In the end, it became a primary vehicle for Christian education and served as a major force in the movement toward universal education.

to my suggestion that perhaps we should just clean, paint, and repair everything and then lock the doors to everyone so that we could always keep things nice. Lightening our load means changing sentimental attachments that make us building protectors rather than practitioners of the presence of Jesus.

Material things are not all that weigh us down. As I review church bulletins and newsletters, I am frequently amazed by how many things even very small churches have going on. Church life is populated by numerous groups, meetings, and activities, many of which support our mission but some of which clutter church life and get in the way of service. We have attachments to our former ways, to subgroups and programs that may have outlived their usefulness. As a Christian educator, I regularly get requests for help increasing Sunday school attendance. How often I hear, "We need children for our Sunday school!"—a statement that betrays the very founding purpose of Sunday school as a way to meet the needs of child laborers. While for many churches Sunday school remains a vibrant, viable ministry, in many others the energy spent trying to keep that program alive might be better used in exploring new ways to reach out to children and to teach the faith. With limited time, energy, and resources, we need to take care that our groups, activities, and programs are streamlined and effective.

It's a big job to continue the ministry of Jesus in the world, so we really need to be able to work together. The Christian church that we have inherited seems to have an excess of dogma; after all, we've had two millennia to develop it. We have argued and broken communion over baptism, the Lord's Supper, marriage and divorce, the Bible, wine versus grape juice, gender roles, dancing, holidays, worship on Saturday versus worship on Sunday . . . the list is endless. And it is an embarrassment. We act as though we have no *thing* in common when, in fact, as we noted above, we have the most important Some*one* in common. Jesus sent his apostles out together and advised them to have their needs met by those who received the gospel (Mark 6:10). We need to stick together and support each other if we are going to be able to fulfill our vital role, and that means letting go of the baggage of hostility over differences.

Yet how do we know which beliefs, activities, groups, or properties are encumbrances and which can help us to be the presence of Jesus? Where can we find the strength to love one another or the wisdom to know where and how to respond to the troubles of this world? For that matter, how can we have the kind of relationship with God that compels us to worship, and how then can we find the tolerance to appreciate each others' celebratory instincts? These, of course, are major tasks and ones that we cannot begin to accomplish without the help of the Holy Spirit.

Trust the Spirit

According to the second chapter of Acts, the church was established by the Spirit during Pentecost, a festival that celebrated the early harvest (Exod. 23:16; Lev. 23:15–21; Deut. 16:9–12). Those who had walked with Jesus represented the early harvest of God's kingdom (Matt. 9:35–38), and as they gathered for the festival, they were given the promised Spirit, who would allow the harvest to continue through their witness (Luke 24:49; Acts 1:8). The Johannine community shares a different version of the story. The Spirit, who would provide comfort and remind them of the truth (John 15–17), was bestowed on the disciples by the breath of the resurrected Jesus as he sent them out into the world (John 20:19–23). Both stories agree that the Spirit is the very presence of Jesus, who sustains the communal life of believers and empowers their mission. We see the Spirit active in the life of the early communities, guiding their witness (Acts 4:8, 31; 6:3–5; 13:2–9; John 15:18–26), bearing fruit (Gal. 5:22–26), gifting and teaching believers (1 Cor. 12–14; Eph. 4; 1 John 2:22; 3:24; 5:6), and making obedience possible (Rom. 8:1–17). The experience of grace, the ability to love, the wisdom to know how and where to reach out to the world, and the strength to maintain fellowship are all made possible by the Spirit.

William Stringfellow identifies discernment as one of the most crucial and most neglected gifts of the Spirit.[16]

> The powers of discernment are held by Saint Paul to be the most necessary to the receipt and effectual use of the many other charismatic gifts (1 Cor. 12). Discernment furnishes the context for other tasks and functions of the people of God. It safeguards against covetousness, pride, trick, exploitation, abuse or dissipation (1 Cor. 13, 14). Morever, discernment represents the fulfillment of the promise of Jesus to his disciples that they would receive authority *and* capability by the Holy Spirit to address and to serve all humanity (John 15:18–26). . . . And discernment is thereafter always evident in practice wherever the Church is alive (see Acts 2:12–21).[17]

Stringfellow proposes that discernment is directly related to the vitality of our celebrations and enables us to rebuke the power of death while nurturing life.[18]

Similarly, David White, director of research for the Youth Theological Initiative at the Candler School of Theology, counsels that "the practice of discernment assumes that God seeks to lead people to greater fullness and faithfulness" while also recognizing that "human sinfulness inhibits God's direction by confusing superficial distractions with our deepest desires to love God and neighbor."[19] He goes on to identify four interconnected movements that can help us turn from superficial distractions and practice discernment in a way that integrates mind, soul, and body. These are listening, acting, understanding, and remembering or dreaming.[20] Trusting the Spirit means being bold enough not only to seek guidance in stillness, prayer, and Scripture, but also to dream together, as did the early Christian communities, that the world might one day know Jesus, and then to act to make that dream come true, discovering as we go what works and what doesn't.

The power of Christian community to form followers of Jesus depends on its authenticity, which is substantiated by our responsiveness, gratitude, grace, communion, and witness. The expression of Christian community that most readily comes to mind is probably the local congregation, which is the primary focus of this book. Christian community has other manifestations, however, all of which have the power to shape Christian identity. These include parachurch organizations, parochial schools, denominations, ecumenical organizations, and of course families.

The Christian Family as Christian Community

In her book *Postmodern Children's Ministry*, children's minister Ivy Beckwith reminds us that the family is the most formative force in the life of a child.

> Family is everything to a child. Family is the first place a child forms and experiences relationships. It is a child's first experience

of community. Family is where she develops her first view and understanding of the world. . . . With that in mind I don't think it's an exaggeration to say that family is the most important arena for a child's spiritual development and soul care.[21]

As the most important arena for the spiritual development of children, family life demands our attention.

While studying at the Franciscan Institute of Saint Bonaventure University in the summer of 1986, I met Sister Angeline (Geline) Joseph Bernardo, a Poor Clare who was visiting from the Philippines. Many at the institute, including me, were drawn to Geline's gentle, loving presence. She and I developed a friendship, and throughout her year at the university, we shared simple meals, long walks through the woods, and contemplative silence. One day I asked her how she came by her loving spirit. I expected her to refer to the many hours of prayer that she kept even while outside the cloister, but instead she said, "I always knew I was deeply loved. I was surrounded in childhood by family and friends who loved me." It would seem incumbent upon Christian parents to make every effort to create homes filled with (per Paul in 1 Cor. 13:4–7) patient, kind, modest, calm, humble, respectful, longsuffering, honest, hopeful, resilient, and joyful love. Sadly, that is not always the case.

We recently had a "parking-lot chat" with a young woman who had just moved into our apartment complex. When she learned that my husband and I are both American Baptist clergy, she remarked, "Oh yeah. My parents are Christians. I was spanked a lot growing up." How sad that the distinguishing characteristic of her life in a Christian household that first came to this woman's mind was regular physical punishment. To judge from my conversations with people raised in churchgoing homes, her experience is far from unique. For many, the phrase *Christian parenting* evokes images of cheerless austerity and a commitment to the misappropriated maxim not to "spare the rod." How can children encounter the God of grace in such a context? Or, more bluntly put, how can salvation be communicated if community life, whether church, denomination, or family, is a hellish experience?

SPARE THE ROD

The phrase "Spare the rod and spoil the child" comes from *Hudibras*, a mock-heroic poem by Samuel Butler about the English Civil War of the seventeenth century. The narrative satirically praises Sir Hudibras, an arrogant, stupid, greedy, and dishonest knight. Part 2 describes a visit to the imprisoned Hudibras by a widow he has been wooing. It is in this section and in reference to squelching romantic feelings that the misused phrase appears:

> What med'cine else can cure the fits
> Of lovers when they lose their wits?
> Love is a boy by poets stil'd;
> Then spare the rod and spoil the child.[22]

The inclination to seek children's obedience as if obeying parents were equivalent to obeying God teeters on the brink of blasphemy. Even with their emphasis on structure and appropriate behavior, the later Pauline communities joined the radical voices of their day in calling for fathers not to be hard on their children (Col. 3:20–21; Eph. 6:1–4), a plea that challenged the prevailing culture's emphasis on obedience. Yet they didn't stop there. Surpassing the moderating voices outside the church and in sharp contrast to the Graeco-Roman household codes, Colossians and Ephesians frame their lists of household conventions within a call for mutual submission (Eph. 5:21), compassion, kindness, lowliness, meekness, patience, forbearance, forgiveness, and love in all relationships (Col. 3:12–14). While the Graeco-Roman codes are addressed to fathers as gods of their households, Colossians and Ephesians raised the status of children by addressing them directly. Additionally, these writings modified obedience with the phrase *in the Lord*, indicating that "parents stand alongside children *under* the Lord."[23] Even among these rule-oriented communities, the witness is clear that there are standards for adults as well as for children, and that those standards do not allow for emotionally or physically bullying children into obedience.

THE EFFECTS OF SPANKING

Numerous studies have confirmed negative long-term consequences of even minimal amounts of corporal punishment.[24]

Effects of spanking noted in childhood include

- aggressive behavior, especially evident two or three years later;
- lowered self-esteem and negative self-image;
- lack of spontaneity, fear of trying new things;
- sadomasochistic tendencies;
- poor performance in school, especially on timed activities;
- limited problem-solving ability;
- higher levels of reactance, the desire to engage in prohibited behaviors; and
- lower scores on intelligence tests.

Effects of spanking noted in adulthood (compared with those not physically punished in childhood) include higher incidence of deviant sexual behavior and psychological disorders.

- A 1995 study by Harriet McMillan of McMaster University in Hamilton, Ontario, reported:
  ○ 30 percent higher incidence of anxiety;
  ○ 50 percent higher incidence of major depression;
  ○ 127 percent higher incidence of alcohol abuse; and
  ○ higher incidence of antisocial behavior.
- A 1987 study by research psychologists Adah Maurer and James S. Wallerstein reported:
  ○ 100 percent of violent inmates at San Quentin Prison in 1987 had experienced extreme physical punishment as children;
  ○ 95 percent of juvenile delinquents had experienced severe or extreme physically punishment; and
  ○ 92 percent of high school dropouts had experienced moderate or severe physical punishment.

We recognize that the skills of Christian marriage are not innate to us, and most churches offer premarital counseling to identify potential problems and teach relational tools. Yet we seem to consider parenting a private matter, adhering to the right of parents to raise children as they see fit. The message of the radical view of children found in the ministry of Jesus and throughout the New Testament testifies to the right of children to be raised in respectful, nurturing environments. Effective Christian education of children requires attention to the experience of the child in the home. As such, we might consider providing preparatory and ongoing parental counseling or classes to help adults learn the skills of gentle parenting.

Christian families have often followed the lead of the church in using even our sacred Scriptures and creedal formulations to oppress children. William Faulkner's *A Light in August* tells the story of a young boy who refuses every effort of his adoptive father to force him to learn his tradition's catechism. Beaten after each refusal to memorize, the child never capitulates, and in his resistance we see an honesty, an integrity, and a sense of self not evident in the dutifully religious parent. In a less extreme example, my favorite television mom, Olivia Walton, often punished her children by making them read the Bible. These fictional accounts bear witness to the common practice of turning the life-giving stories and summaries of our faith into vehicles of coerced discipleship. In so doing, we violate our traditions and diminish their value for the Christian education endeavor. Only when respected and embodied in the life of the community can our traditions play a crucial role in nurturing followers of Jesus. In the next chapter we will turn our attention to this role.

Exercises for Individuals or Groups

1. Spend some time in personal reflection on your childhood, bringing to mind times that you felt truly loved. Read 1 Corinthians 13:4–7, and during the next few days note how people use the word *love* and compare their actions with this definition.

2. In the early communities, the efficacy of sharing the gospel was revealed in the quality of the life of the community. Either privately or in a small group, spend some time honestly assessing your faith community. In what ways does it bear the marks of authenticity?

3. Consider the place of children in your church and your family. How does your situation align with the view of children offered in this chapter? Do you feel any discomfort with some of what's been said here in regard to children? If so, spend some time reflecting on that discomfort or discussing it with others. What information do these feelings offer about your experiences, your assumptions, and your expectations?

4. Invite your pastor or other church leaders to explain your church's practices of preparation for marriage and for the dedication or baptism of children. What do the distinctions between these practices suggest about your church's perspectives on parenting? How do you think people would react to the suggestion of preparatory counseling for parenting?

5. Referring to your church's bulletins, newsletters, and constitution, work together in a group to map how your energy, time, and other resources are used. How many activities, groups, and beliefs support your mission to the world? Do you see any excess baggage? What emotional attachments might make it difficult to lighten the load?

7

Guided by Tradition

That conceptual inheritance, or beliefs and belief systems, makes no sense at all apart from a particular historical community, with its story, symbols, habitual ways of thinking and doing. That is to say, beliefs cannot be perceived as logical systems in isolation from lived reality. Nor is ideology to be viewed in the negative sense of ideas developed as weapons or rationalizations for use by individuals or societies for selfish ends. Rather ideology is viewed positively, as the humble, heuristic, intentional effort to make sense of things.

—SARA LITTLE, *TO SET ONE'S HEART*[1]

We stand today as followers of Jesus because the first communities of believers preserved the tradition that guides Christian discipleship. The term *tradition* refers to the truths that define us, and for the faith community, this includes confessions, creeds, denominational decrees, mission statements, and of course, the Bible, which has unique standing and authority. In this chapter, we will begin with a look at the nature and role of our tradition and then move on to consider how we go about preserving this tradition for discipleship.

A Live, Living, and Lived Tradition

The presence of Jesus, which was central to the self-understanding of all the early Christian communities, was communicated through their traditions. In that sense, the traditions were "live," bearing with them the very presence of the living and exalted Christ. The traditions of the earliest Christian communities included the Hebrew Scriptures (there was no New Testament yet), the Jesus traditions, summaries of faith, and correspondence from the communities' founders. According to James Dunn, these traditions were shared in a context in which:

> Each community and each new generation accepted a responsibility laid upon it (implicitly or explicitly by the Spirit) to interpret the received tradition afresh and in relation to its own situation and needs.[2]

The shared traditions were a unifying aspect of the early communities, while the application of those traditions diverged significantly as the gospel spread across geography and generations. The traditions were preserved, transmitted, and reframed for new contexts. They were also brought to life within the communities as the members lived them out in their relationships and structures. The traditions were, therefore, living stories of faith, interpreted by the power of the Spirit for each new setting. Finally, the traditions were at work in the communities, forming and transforming the lives of individuals and the life of the community itself. Christian tradition is a dynamic, pneumatic, and embodied tradition that communicates the presence of Jesus, is interpreted through the Spirit, and is lived out among believers.

Scripture as Authoritative Story

Formed through a long and somewhat complex process, what now stands as the Christian Bible (with some differences among our communions) is a compilation of components of the traditions of the earliest communities—the Hebrew Scriptures, precreedal formulae, collected narratives and sayings of Jesus, and writings of founders and leaders of the communities. The Bible has been approached in a variety of ways, including as an authoritative history, as a system of official doctrines and concepts, and as a collection of ancient documents to be scrutinized with the tools of scholarship. While each of these approaches has helped us appropriate the witness of Scripture, each also risks missing the Bible's fundamental narrative character.[3]

FORMATION OF THE BIBLE

It took well over a thousand years for all the books of the Bible to be individually written down, and even more years before those books were brought together into what we know as our Bible. The stories of Scripture began as oral traditions, some of which were passed down for centuries before taking written form. The first written forms of stories, songs, and prophecies that would become part of the Hebrew Scriptures were written around 1800 BCE, and the remainder were written and collected over a period of centuries.

The earliest manuscripts of the Bible have been lost to history. Our current Bible rests on copies of copies of copies. It is supposed that the Hebrew Scriptures were being collected as early as 400 BCE, and the oldest Greek translation of the Hebrew Scriptures is the Septuagint, which was completed between 300 BCE and 100 BCE. The process of determining an official version of the contents of the Hebrew Scriptures, however, was not completed until nearly one hundred years after Jesus at the Council of Jamnia.

The earliest written documents of our New Testament are the early letters of Paul. It was not until about the year 65 that the stories and sayings of Jesus began to be gathered and written down. For three centuries, church leaders argued about which writings should be treated as Scripture. A list provided in 367 by Athanasius, the bishop of Alexandria, lists the books that are currently in the Protestant New Testament; however, debate about particular books, such as James and Revelation, continued into the sixteenth century.[4]

Scripture is ultimately a collection of stories, parts of stories, letters, and liturgical formulations that come together under the inspiration of the Holy Spirit to create a guiding narrative for Christian discipleship. As a unit, the Bible tells of God's activity in history and of human response to that activity. Each piece of Scripture, whether book, chapter, or single verse, is best understood in the context of that broader biblical narrative and in its own unique narrative context. The

Bible and its component parts become authoritative as they guide our narrative, transforming the stories of who we are in that same dynamic, Spirit-led process that was present in the early communities, as suggested in Marianne Sawicki's discussion of "God's word":

> The concept of "God's word," then, points both to the Bible and to Jesus Christ. . . . That antique book, and that historical individual . . . do indeed present communication from God to human beings; but such communication is not confined to them. We think of God's Word also as a process which continues every day in every human life. For a communication to be successful, it must be received. God said everything there was to say in Jesus; God's communication cannot be completed until the last human being in history has responded to God's invitation. In this sense, the Bible is still becoming the word of God for each person who picks it up and receives its message.[5]

The authority of Scripture is revealed as we live it out in our individual lives, the community of faith, and the world. In living out the tradition, we become part of the ongoing saga of God's activity in human history. Our task, therefore, is not to defend Scripture to others as an inerrant universal authority, but to welcome its story into our story, embracing its witness without apology as our authoritative tradition and preserving it for future generations.

Of course, some may argue against my assertion that the Bible is primarily story. We've certainly not always treated it that way, even when its narrative nature is obvious. Consider, for example, our treatment of the Exodus. This dramatic story of a group of slaves rescued from Egypt to become a nation unto the Lord is frequently reduced to a list of rules to be imposed on generations and cultures far removed, without any regard for the narrative context that gives meaning to those decrees. Even those elements of Scripture that don't seem to be narrative are part of the storied tradition of our faith. The writings of Paul, for example, are letters, of course, but they are letters embedded in the story of the gospel's spread among particular groups in the reaches of the Roman Empire. Although Scripture is our primary guiding tradition, other historic traditions have varying degrees of authority within our faith communities. They too have their stories.

Confessions, Creeds, Catechisms, and Their Stories

As we saw in the early Christian communities, structure and codification of beliefs were a response to the rise of internal threats and to increased distance from the eyewitnesses of Jesus. In his discussion of the life settings of early confessional formulae, James Dunn concludes that the early communities did not confess Jesus's ideas, his faith, or his teachings. Instead they confessed Jesus as the one present in the community, while maintaining a vital link between that exalted one and the historical Jew of Galilee, "the present author of life, justification, power, *Jesus*, the Jesus who was, *is*, now is and continues to be Christ, Son of God, Lord."[6] Further, Dunn proffers that the confessions of the early communities were diverse because they were used by Christians who were different from one another and who expressed their faith in very different circumstances through formulations that "lay bare the distinctiveness of the faith confessed in *different particular situations*."[7]

Even summaries of the faith, such as confessions, creeds, and catechisms, are narrative in that the stories of their development place them in particular contexts, which, when understood, can help us more accurately understand their meaning. This is true of the precreedal formulations found within the New Testament[8] and also of later formulations that have historically been authoritative for the church. For example, the Nicene Creed is a product of a theological debate and the church's dramatically changed circumstances under the Emperor Constantine. Up until the time of Constantine's adoption (or exploitation, depending on one's perspective) of the faith, Christianity suffered varying degrees of persecution. One of the most intense periods of persecution was at the hands of Constantine's predecessor, Diocletian. Those difficult years also saw the development of two divergent understandings of Jesus based on the influential teaching of the presbyter Origen (ca. 185–255 CE). Origen had written that since God was eternally existent and Jesus was the only-begotten son, God could never have existed without having generated the son. One understanding drawn from Origen's thought stressed the oneness of the Son with the Father as co-equal and co-eternal. The other understanding emphasized the distinction of the Son from—and his subordination to—the Father. Conflict between the holders of these conceptions broke out over a preacher named Arius, who, in protest to his bishop's assertion that "God is always; the Son is always," claimed that although the Son had a beginning, God was without beginning.[9] Seeing the potential of a unified church to support his hard-won unification of the empire, Constantine summoned the Council of Nicaea in 325 CE to settle the matter. After violent debate, the council agreed to a creed that was a modified version (revised in part with language provided by Constantine, who presided over the gathering) of one offered by the moderate Eusebius of Caesarea. This formulation, known as the Nicene Creed, is still in use today.

Even those communions, such as my own, that claim a commitment to the Bible alone as their authority do rely on other sources as secondary authorities. One such source is the community itself, which guides the use of Scripture, a phenomenon discussed by womanist scholar Renita J. Weems in a compendium on African American biblical interpretation:

> Further, how one reads or interprets the Bible depends in large part on which interpretative community one identifies with at any given time.... In fact, the interpretative community with which one identifies will have a lot to say about what "reading strategy" one will adopt. For, in the end, it is one's interpretative community that tends to regulate which reading strategies are authoritative for the reader and what ought to be the reader's predominant interests.[10]

Among the ways in which the community authorizes reading strategies is through summary interpretations, which, while not granted the same status in Bible-only traditions as in more liturgical traditions, do provide parameters for belief. I recall, for example, during my summers as a counselor at a Bible Club camp, the children reciting "God is omniscient, omnipotent, and omnipresent." This summary of belief in God served as an unofficial yet authoritative creed. Likewise, the premillennial dispensational doctrine outlined by Cyrus Scofield in his reference Bible[11] served as an authoritative summary of the faith for this group, which would strongly assert a commitment to the Bible as the sole authority for Christian life.

Historic creeds, confessions, catechisms, and formalized doctrines were all developed in response to specific issues and circumstances. As such, they emphasize particular aspects of the faith and can be misunderstood outside the actual situations they addressed. Knowing the story behind these faith formulations helps us to understand them and to determine their usefulness for our contemporary contexts.

The Power of Story and the Power of the Storyteller

Being and nurturing disciples of Jesus means preserving the living tradition that guides us. In doing so, we both share the story of Christianity and become a part of that ongoing story. We noted above the power of our sacred narratives to make Jesus present and to shape individuals and communities. Story is powerful because it touches the mind, the heart, and the will. The compelling nature of story is evident everywhere. Novels become best sellers because readers are impassioned by them, and moviegoers can leave theaters enraged about injustice, in tears over the death of fictional characters, or holding their sides in laughter over scenes long past. Our tradition has a power beyond the power of narrative, however, because these stories of faith were inspired in their formulation and recording and continue to be inspired in their retelling (2 Tim. 3:16). The power inherent in narrative also means that anyone who tells or retells the story exercises power.

Throughout this book I have offered stories from my own experience, both to clarify what I want to say and to make use of the power of narrative. I chose each story in hopes of having an impact on readers. As I wrote chapter 6, for instance, I imagined readers responding to the Valentine's Day flower story in a variety of ways, some sharing my anger and others feeling defensive (a first step toward reconsidering assumptions) about teaching children the niceties of polite society. I told each story in a particular way, emphasizing some aspects, ignoring others, and always from my own perspective. Storytellers exercise power by selecting particular stories to tell and by deciding how to tell them. This is also true in the telling of our sacred stories. Terence Copley, professor of educational studies at Oxford University, reminds us of the power that lies not only in religious stories but also in those who retell those stories:

It is evident that in religion as in other spheres, story has immense power. . . . It is equally evident that in the pulpit or the classroom the storyteller adds, alters, deletes, and in that sense becomes part of the story in its present form. This is much more than a matter of hermeneutics, or an awareness that there are ethical issues in presenting history as one form of story. For although all stories must be edited and interpreted, it is clear that some can be transformed, even hijacked, into something quite different from the experience or event that led to the first telling.[12]

The power of our sacred stories and the power inherent in storytelling requires that we approach preserving our tradition with absolute humility, following the lead of those who preserved that tradition for us. So now we look to the early Christian communities for guidance on the question "How do we preserve a living tradition?"

Know the Tradition

Preserving our tradition, of course, requires knowing our tradition. In the earliest Christian gatherings, the stories of faith were shared through instruction in the Hebrew Scriptures and the Jesus tradition, hymn singing, prayer, spontaneous confession, symbols, and rituals. The life of those first-century followers also became a part of the tradition that now guides us when preserved correspondence to them from leaders, such as Paul, became part of our canon. As centuries passed, our forebears in the faith suffered and even died to make the Bible available in the language of everyday people. How sad it is that so many of us are biblically illiterate—both of Bible content and of how this tradition came to us.

Learn the Story of the Story

One of my guilty pleasures is watching "Wife Swap," a show that I doubt has any redemptive value at all but that, for some inexplicable reason, draws me in. For the uninitiated, this "reality" show has wives swapping households for two weeks. To create drama (and apparently to traumatize innocent children), the producers select two extreme and contradictory participants for each swap— for example, trading the mom of an urban, atheist, vegan family with that of a rural "God-fearing" family of hunters. Once they even paired apparently divergent Christian households (extremely educated liberals with extremely uneducated fundamentalists) whose superficial differences of doctrine were obscured by their actual and operative shared qualities of infantilism, self-absorption, and self-righteousness. (The Christian witness may never recover.)

In one episode, an Orthodox Jewish mother entered into discussion with her "new" family's fundamentalist Christian grandmother. When the Jewish woman began to cite a text from the Hebrew Bible, the grandmother interjected, "Is this the official authorized and inerrant King James Bible we're talking about?" When the grandmother inherited the biblical tradition, she apparently hadn't been given the story *of* that tradition, which would have clued her in to the fact the Bible is not a rulebook that magically dropped out of the sky in the king's English. In fact, she might have learned that her centuries-old "only" authoritative version was profoundly progressive in its day and reflected a commitment to honoring our tradition through the best scholarly tools of the time and to making that tradition available in everyday language. Responsible knowledge of the Bible includes knowing its content and knowing the story of its becoming available to all believers as a print resource. Knowing that story can also give us confidence to speak to our day, knowing that the same Spirit that was at work in the Bible's formation is still at work, empowering us and guiding us as we seek to interpret it for a new day.

Recite the Story

An obvious but easily overlooked distinction between first-century Christians and ourselves is that they did not have personal Bibles to read. While each synagogue had a chest in which the scrolls of the Law were kept to be read aloud, the Jesus tradition circulated in oral form. The early communities heard these guiding stories through

THE ENGLISH BIBLE

The official translation of the Bible in the Western (Roman Catholic) church since the fifth century has been Jerome's Latin Vulgate. While several scholars translated select books of the Bible from the Vulgate into English, it was not until the fourteenth century that an entire English version was completed by John Wycliffe.

The invention of movable type in 1455 by Johann Gutenberg and the Protestant Reformation, which began in Germany in 1517, laid the groundwork for having Bible translations in modern languages, based not on the Latin but on older Greek and Hebrew manuscripts. Martin Luther, a German priest and voice of the Reformation, completed a German translation in 1534, and following suit in the commitment to making Scripture accessible to those who could not read Latin, William Tyndale created the first English New Testament based on Greek and Hebrew manuscripts. Having to flee Germany to England because of official hostility to his work, Tyndale was unable to complete his translation of the Old Testament. He was eventually tried for heresy and burned at the stake.

While reading the works of Wycliffe and Tyndale was forbidden by church leaders, other English versions were developed and distributed by the church. The most influential of these was the King James Bible (1611), which James I authorized fifty-four scholars to produce in the English of the day. The translation, which was based on both the oldest manuscripts available at the time and previous English versions, was revised in 1881 and 1885. The discovery in the nineteenth century of many biblical manuscripts more ancient than those on which the King James Version was based led to the development of numerous modern translations, including the Revised Standard Version (1952), the New Revised Standard Version (1999), and the American Standard Version (1901), which incorporated earlier revisions of the King James. The process of translating the Bible continues today, helped by ongoing discovery of ancient manuscripts.[13]

preaching, recited prayers, confessions (which were frequently sung as hymns), and rituals and symbols. Contemporary Christian education recognizes the importance of reading and hearing our guiding story but tends to overlook the power that rituals and symbols also have to "speak" that tradition. Many of our rituals are ancient ones, and while first-century Jesus followers understood their import, the further removed we are from the Jesus event, the more important it is to couple our rituals with the stories that give them meaning. Celebrating rituals in isolation from the stories that ground them can lead to aberrant understandings of our tradition.

Several years ago, a few days before I was to serve as supply preacher at a nearby Presbyterian church, I received a call from a member of the session (congregational governing board) asking me if I'd be willing to baptize a baby during the service. He explained that the couple had recently adopted a child from China and were in the area visiting the wife's family. The parents had met with the session, which had approved the baptism, even though the couple lived in another state and were not members of any church. The session members felt assured that the couple was planning to join a Presbyterian church in the town where they lived. Although I'm American Baptist, my ordination was recognized by the local presbytery, and with the session's approval I agreed to do the baptism. I called the mother to clarify matters, and when I asked about their plans to raise the child in the church, she responded that although they might join a church, it wouldn't be Presbyterian. I asked why she wanted the child baptized, and she responded, "Well if, God forbid, anything were to happen to her, we don't want her to go to hell." Astonished, I caught my breath and did my best to explain a Christian understanding of a gracious God and a Presbyterian understanding of baptism, after which she reconfirmed their interest in having the child baptized in the church where her mother was a longtime member. I followed up with a call to my session contact. He expressed surprise at what I'd found out but reiterated the session's support for the baptism, at which point I concluded that: (1) the session hadn't done its job very well, (2) the session's support for the baptism was more about the grandmother's place in the church, and (3) I was in a difficult position. My deliberations about how to proceed were influenced by an experience I'd had fifteen years earlier.

During what I thought was a casual conversation, a longtime member of the church I was serving wondered about having her son's new baby baptized "sometime" when they came to visit from a neighboring state. I was surprised that a lifelong Baptist would suggest baptizing a baby, and instead of addressing whatever need lay beneath the request, I offered an explanation of the Baptist understanding of baptism. The woman became annoyed, but it wasn't until the mother of the child accompanied her to worship the following Sunday—and after I had received angry phone calls from church members (word traveled fast)—that I understood that what I thought was a general inquiry about baptism was apparently a specific request for a dedication service. The baby was a beautiful little girl with black tresses and a sweet smile, but she saw difficulties early on in her little life. Before her first birthday, her unmarried parents ended their relationship, and soon after, it was discovered that she was deaf. That incident has stayed with me, and even though neither baptism nor a traditional dedication service fit the situation, I often wish I had thought to offer a ritual that, at the very least, said, "This beautiful child is a child of God. May all who touch her life help her to know God's grace." And so, with the memory of that lapse in the back of my mind, I worked with the parents of the adopted child to create a ritual that reflected their beliefs and at which I could officiate with integrity.

No doubt some readers are cringing right now, thinking I acted inappropriately in either or both situations. I tell this story simply to make the point that our rituals are grounded in our beliefs, and that conducting them apart from the stories that give them meaning can lead to grave misunderstandings. On the other hand, when we participate in rituals that reflect beliefs that the participants don't really hold, we communicate that our beliefs don't really matter. Such activities dishonor our tradition.

Honor the Tradition

We honor our tradition when we participate in authentic rituals that tell the stories of our actual beliefs. We also honor our tradition when we trust it to do its work in our lives and in the lives of those with whom we share it.

Trust the Story

I spent several years working as an editor of Christian education materials. Routinely such resources have a section dedicated to paraphrasing the text and, especially in children's materials, retelling Bible stories. Just as routinely writers of curriculum materials take liberties with the stories, creating versions that frequently dictate the meaning for learners. Russ Dalton, associate professor of Christian education at Brite Divinity School, found similar practices in his analysis of children's Bibles.

Having surveyed hundreds of Bible storybooks, Dalton noted the widespread practice of revising Bible stories in ways that eliminated ambiguities, contracted meaning, created unblemished heroes or heroines, and reduced the stories to simple morality tales. Focusing on the stories of Noah and Jonah, Dalton identified multiple examples of Bible stories retold in ways that teach moral lessons or specific virtues. One example among the many he noted in the hundreds of publications he reviewed came in the retelling of the Noah story in *The Beginners Bible Tales of Virtue: A Book of Right and Wrong*:

> Noah worked every day on the ark. He worked for many years. His sons helped him. Sometimes it was easy. Sometimes it was hard. Sometimes it was fun. Sometimes it was boring. But they knew they were doing God's special work. Noah did everything God told him to do. He was happy because his work made his family strong.[14]

This revamped story, which appears to intend to teach the value of hard work, evidences the purpose operative in the collection and apparent in the title phrase "tales of virtue." The author is far from alone in her approach.[15] While work and other virtues are valuable for children to learn, narrowing the message of the stories of our tradition to these qualities necessitates altering the text. Such practices demonstrate a (no doubt unconscious) mistrust of the Bible and willingness to supplant biblical authority with one's own authoritative intentions. Further, as Dalton points out, these renderings of the stories eliminate gaps and ambiguities that are a crucial component of the stories of the Hebrew Bible (and presumably of many of our New Testament stories):

> These gaps are the parts of the story that are not filled in by the storyteller, but left to the imagination of the audience. . . . By engaging these gaps, readers can participate in the story and can actively find and create meaning relevant to their own context and experience.[16]

Honoring our tradition means allowing the stories to stand, trusting them to do their work, and resisting the temptation to fill in their silent places for others. It is important to note that the gaps in the stories create the spaces where we can enter the stories and allow them to read us and our situations. They invite us to question the stories, knowing that they are imperturbable purveyors of truth, not only for us but for others. The process of imagining ourselves into the stories helps us find meaning with our hearts as well as our minds. Honoring the tradition means trusting the story and trusting that the One who is made present to us in the story guides each of us in making that story a part of our lives.

Apply the Story

Our primary authoritative tradition, the Bible, is an admittedly long and complex book with a fairly complicated history. The institutional church's early history of preserving the Bible's contents for an ecclesiastical elite, along with the more recent practice of leaving biblical study to an academic elite, has created a culture of insecurity that often keeps everyday folk away from our sacred texts. Yet we needn't be afraid of the Bible. The Bible's size and complexity are among its attributes. All of us, including those who sequester themselves in the halls of academia, can spend our lifetimes searching its treasures yet never run out of new life-giving territory to explore. Our feelings of intimidation regarding the Bible and our ignorance of its content can easily be dispelled simply by opening its pages and reading. Most of us already possess and practice many of the skills necessary for responsible reading of the Scriptures.

It might be helpful to remember the narrative character of our tradition—there is nothing intimidating about a good story. We all have lifetimes of experience hearing and reading stories. The skills we've acquired through those experiences provide a strong foundation for closing the gap between us and the contexts out of which our sacred story emerged. When we open a book, we are inclined to know a little bit about it before we begin reading: Is it a biography or science fiction? When was it written? Who wrote it and why? We note by layout and language if individual sections of the book are poems or letters or fables. If, as we read, we come across words we don't understand, we look them up in a dictionary. When an unfamiliar concept or historical incident is mentioned, we check with a knowledgeable friend or do a little research. Terminology that is unique or used in specialized ways is defined by how those terms are used within the story itself (for example, who could know the meaning of "Hogwarts," "muggles," "winzengamot," or "pensieve" outside of *Harry Potter*?). These skills, which come quite naturally to us, are the very skills needed to uncover the truths in the tradition we hope to preserve.

These truths are truths *we live by*. The early communities applied their beliefs to their lives, interpreting them for their contexts in light of the general principle of love (1 Cor. 8:1b). The stories of faith that the early Jesus followers shared were called on to answer the practical questions of Jesus's identity, their identity in relationship to Jesus, and how to live in the world in light of those two realities. It was in addressing these day-to-day questions that the tradition was brought to life—literally, brought into the realm of everyday living on this earth. Prosaic questions were rarely bypassed with the ethereal theologizing we often find in our communities. Many contemporary churches, for example, have loftily worded mission statements into which went many hours of deliberation. Most of those statements seem impossible to put into practice, though, speaking as they do in grand abstractions about such things as "endeavoring to cooperate in God's redemptive plan for the world."[17] Seldom do these statements address questions such as: How do we make sure everyone gets a fair share of our limited food supplies? (Acts 6:1–7); Can we do business with people who have beliefs different from ours? (1 Cor. 8:1–13); or, What do we do about stupid people? (1 Pet. 2:15).

Practical interpretation of our tradition brings that early story into our story by addressing the matters we really care about in ways that have meaning for us. I remember in the 1990s weeping every time I heard Eric Clapton's "Tears in Heaven." The song touched me deeply, since I had recently watched as my mother succumbed to complications from the flu. I discovered that I was not alone in my response to Clapton's ruminations on the death of his young son, and always analytical, I pondered why those lyrics had such a profound impact on so many. I concluded that it was the real, heart-wrenching questions the song expressed that stirred me—and still bring me to tears today. I didn't care about erudite speculations about the spatiality and physicality of heaven. My pain was not eased by the platitudes of adherents of "the Oprah school of theology" who assured me that "everything happens for a reason." I wanted to hear that, in the mysteries of divine grace, my mother and I would somehow always know one another. I wanted to be assured that there was a day ahead when again I'd hear her speak my name. I needed to be reminded that God really is good, that Jesus made absolutely, undeniably clear that love conquers even death, and that I needn't let my heart be troubled (John 14:1, 27). These were the live questions of my heart, and such questions can be addressed only by a living tradition.

Honoring our living tradition means sharing the stories *and* providing the tools for interpreting and applying the tradition, tools for "rightly explaining the word of truth" (2 Tim. 2:15). I mentioned above that I think most of us already operate with the skills needed to understand the Bible. The three tools that appear to be lacking are an understanding of how that tradition came to be, the permission to interpret the tradition in light of its history, and the confidence to apply it to our contemporary situations. As we honor our tradition, we trust the stories and also the Spirit, who guides us *and* others in appropriating those stories for their lives. In so doing, we recognize that the tradition is shared property.

Pass On the Tradition

To authentically be the divine/human gospel, our tradition must continually be welcomed into the human experience, proclaimed through word and prophetic-symbolic acts to new and potential disciples of Jesus. The early Christian communities shared the message of God's kingdom during worship of the gathered community, which we discussed above, and through proclamation. According to James Dunn, the precreedal confessions that we find in the New Testament were primarily used in proclamation to those who were not followers of Jesus.[18] Preservation of our living tradition, then, requires giving it away, sharing our sacred story beyond the walls of the church.

Proclaim the Story in Meaningful Ways

For the early Christian communities, sharing the tradition involved both introducing some unfamiliar concepts to new audiences and presenting its truths in the language and concepts of those groups. This meant distilling essential elements of the tradition and practicing discernment to avoid "confusing superficial distractions with our deepest desire to love God and neighbor."[19] Summaries of our beliefs help us to frame our tradition for proclamation in new circumstances. When using historic formulations, even those found in Scripture, we need to be sure that they still say what they said in their formation. In his discussion of early confessional formulae, James Dunn reminds us that unless the gospel is contextualized, it is not the gospel, that each confession was important in its own sphere because "each was [presumably] the most *relevant* and *meaningful* expression of Christianity in that situation." He goes on to warn:

> Confessions framed in one context do not remain the same when that context changes. New situations call forth new confessions. A Christianity that ceases to develop new confessional language ceases to confess its faith to the contemporary world.[20]

That is, phrases used at one place and time in history may have different meanings in other places and times and so may no longer accurately express the tradition. Developing new summaries of faith using language, concepts, and imagery that have meaning for contemporary audiences brings our tradition to life for a new day and for new people. The primary confessions of Jesus in the early communities, for example, went from "Jesus is Messiah" to "Jesus is the Son of God" to "Jesus is Lord"—changes in wording and concepts that communicated "old" beliefs for new settings.

Reframing the truths that we live by in language, concepts, and symbols that have meaning to new generations demonstrates the dynamic character of that truth, which, as Sara Little reminds us,

> is not a tightly knit, logical system of belief, not a static body of propositions that may pose as absolute truth, not even truth that is experienced and "known" through intuition or mystical moments of awareness. What is meant, rather, is the idea of truth, and how it functions in our lives. Truth is before us as mystery, reality, and the wonder of that which is transcendent, which stands as a reference corrective, and source or power to those who seek to be conformed unto it.[21]

Sharing our tradition and opening ourselves up to new ways of expressing that guiding story demonstrate that we are not passing *down* the tradition, but passing *on* the tradition.

Surrender the Story

The spread of Christianity from a distinctly Jewish sect to a faith that included Gentiles was dependent on the trust and humility of those first Jewish followers of Jesus. As Christian disciples, we are indebted to Judaism for housing within itself the sect that became Christianity as well as for giving us the foundation for that faith. The early followers of the Way preserved the tradition by letting go of the tradition. They surrendered the story to new people, to new ways of expressing it, to new understandings, and to new applications. What greater testament is there to the power of Jesus's resurrection and to the strength of the tradition that a people could so courageously entrust their sacred story to people so different from themselves? And how sad that some of those who received that gift later used it to denigrate the givers and to break fellowship with them.

As we proclaim our story and allow its power to form new disciples of Jesus, we find that the tradition is no longer *ours*. This is true of any knowledge that we presume to hand on to others. Consider, for example, how we approach children who are learning the alphabet. We ask, "Do you know *your* ABCs?" When they are learned, they are no longer *our* ABCs, but *their* ABCs, a shared foundation with which learners have now entered into relationship. When we preserve our tradition, it ceases to be our private domain but becomes the rightful property of others. This reality was affirmed by the Second Vatican Council of the Roman Catholic Church:

> There is growth in the understanding of the realities and the words which have been handed down. This happens through the contemplation and study made by believers, who treasure these things in their hearts (cf. Lk. 2:19, 51), through understanding of spiritual things they experience, and through the preaching of those who have received through episcopal succession the sure gift of truth. For, as the centuries succeed one another, the church constantly moves forward toward the fullness of divine truth until the words of God reach their complete fulfillment.[22]

Our guiding tradition is like the love that is housed within it. The more we give it away, the stronger and more vital it grows. After all, it is a *living* tradition. We need to be prepared, then, for young believers and new believers to bring the sacred story to life *for us* by framing it and interpreting it in new ways. In the end, as we seek to nurture disciples of Jesus, we will find them nurturing us.

Exercises for Individuals or Groups

1. Spend some time in personal reflection thinking about how you've encountered the living tradition of Christianity. Then either privately or in discussion groups, consider the ways in which your church currently tells the sacred stories of our faith.
2. Over a period of weeks, pay attention to the traditions other than the Bible that your church treats as authoritative. These may be subtle and can be as complex as denominational statements or as simple as the way your church traditionally handles shared meals.

3. All communities—denominations, congregations, and families—have rituals. Some are formal, such as ordination, baptism, and weddings. Others are informal, like how meetings are started or how birthdays are celebrated. Identify and critically assess the rituals of the Christian communities you are a part of. In what ways do those rituals communicate the beliefs of the community? In what ways are they misunderstood? What steps could be taken to make your rituals authentic rituals?

4. Review the curriculum materials your church is currently using. How do they approach the Bible? Are there retellings of Bible stories? If so, compare those versions to the stories as they appear in Scripture.

Conclusion

A Lesson Plan for Christian Education

The way is unutterably hard, and at every moment we are in danger of straying from it. If we regard this way as one we follow in obedience to an external command, if we are afraid of ourselves all the time, it is indeed an impossible way. But if we behold Jesus Christ going on before step by step, if we only look to him and follow him, step by step, we shall not go astray. . . . For he is himself the way, the narrow way and the strait gate. He, and he alone, is our journey's end.

—DIETRICH BONHOEFFER, *THE COST OF DISCIPLESHIP* [1]

We began our journey together with visits to the first-century roots of Christian discipleship in the ministry of Jesus and the life of the primitive Christian communities. We discovered that the work of Jesus was a prophetic ministry in which he proclaimed God's kingdom through stories, debate, prophetic-symbolic acts, and the life he shared with his followers. We saw that the call to follow Jesus was a call to leave behind old self-definitions to be redefined by relationship with Jesus, a call that presumed community among those who responded to it.

We found that as generations of Jesus followers worked out how to continue his ministry after his death and later, after the death of those who knew him personally, they took some very different paths. While sharing a belief in the ongoing presence of the resurrected Jesus, they diverged in how they lived out that belief and how they framed the message for new places and times. We learned from the early communities that the church remains or becomes strong by having deep roots and flexible branches, by holding on to what is essential and having the courage to adapt to new situations. At the end of that first leg of our journey, I offered the following summary understanding of discipleship: Discipleship is a way of being grounded in vocation, nurtured within community, and guided by tradition.

In the introduction to this book I contended that this is a time for repentance: a time for turning from our victim mentality and toward the unique hope of this day for Christian discipleship. The categories of turning from and turning toward provide a helpful rubric for reviewing some of the territory covered in section 2.

Turning from:	*Turning toward:*
• Discipleship imposed from the outside	• Discipleship growing from within
• Discipleship dependent on human will	• Discipleship dependent on Jesus
• Magic, pretense, and rigidity	• Relationship, authenticity, and responsiveness
• Self-justification and self-righteousness	• Grace-filled and gracious lives
• Elitism, protectionism, and discord	• Radical community
• Coercion, manipulation, and judgment	• Prophetic-symbolic presence
• Biblical illiteracy and misuse	• Knowing and honoring the sacred story
• Marginalization of children	• Defining and organizing community around children

Summarizing the Hope

A second rubric, which is useful for summarizing the hope uncovered in section 2, is a lesson plan. Educators often strategize their endeavors through lesson plans, which help them map where they want to go, how they plan to get there, and how to evaluate their efforts. Lesson plans presume the who and where of the educational enterprise and include the following main elements:

- A goal, which presents the broad purpose or aim of the educational enterprise
- Objectives that describe intermediate aims in service to the goal
- A description of methods and materials that will be used
- A plan for assessing whether the goal and objectives were met

I offer the following suggested lesson plan for Christian education.

Who

The teachers include Jesus, who is present through his Spirit; designated teachers who speak the language of grace, know the tradition, and practice authentic discipleship; the entire community *as a community*; and designated learners who teach those who presume to teach them. The learners include the teachers, faith communities as communities, and new and future followers of Jesus.

Where

Educational ministry is carried out in the gathered community—in churches, denominations, ecumenical groups, families, and other Christian institutions—and in the world where God is present and the church is active.

Goal

The overarching goal of Christian education is to nurture relationship with Jesus through which people are transformed and empowered to reclaim the vocations of renewed relationship with God, themselves, and the world.

Objectives

Participants will
- encounter the presence of God in the gathered community, through worship, the tradition, the structures, and human interactions;

- recognize the language of grace in the community, in the tradition, and in creation;
- speak the language of grace to themselves, to their Christian brothers and sisters, and to the world;
- celebrate the stories of our sacred tradition and express an understanding of how that tradition came to be;
- interpret those stories and develop formulations of the faith using language, concepts, and modes of expression that have meaning for them;
- experiment with discernment through prayer, meditation, and stillness;
- express an understanding of the stories behind the rituals of the community and help develop rituals that authentically and explicitly reflect their beliefs;
- observe the culture and identify areas of need, places where God is at work, and new ways to share the message of the kingdom; and
- contribute to the faith community by reframing Christian beliefs, creating new rituals, and applying the stories of the faith in new ways.

Methods and Materials

Methods will include
- participation in the life of an authentic, radical, and responsive Christian community;
- service to the world, especially to those on the margins of society;
- hearing, reciting, retelling, and seeing the stories of our faith at work; and
- practice in interpretation, meditation, and prayer.

The content will include
- Scripture;
- ancient, contemporary, formal, and informal creedal summaries and confessions;
- old hymns and new songs;
- traditional and newly imagined symbols;

- unpolished stories of historic and contemporary heroes and heroines of the faith;
- stories from the world around us, especially of those who are marginalized and powerless; and
- the space and freedom to live out discipleship in ways that make sense for participants' lives and are true to their callings from God.

Assessment

The barometer for effectiveness of our educational efforts will be threefold:

- authenticity, integrity, and grace in the life of the learner;
- enhanced faithfulness, confidence, and grace in the life of Christian community; and
- clarity of witness to the kingdom through the palpable presence of Jesus in the world.

The evaluation process is an active-reflective one in which we carry out our efforts with an attitude of continual reassessment, always open to modifying our approaches in light of our results and the guidance of the Spirit.

Exercises for Individuals or Groups

1. Develop a plan for personal and communal repentance. Spend some time paying attention to practices of your church that hinder authentic discipleship and the ways in which you participate in those practices. Think about how you might revise or replace those practices. Consider developing a ritual to mark your commitment to repentance.
2. The Christian faith is a responsive faith, and at its most effective, education is a contextual process. While always having some foundational similarities, successful formation of followers of Jesus will look different in different settings.

Modify the lesson plan above, using language, concepts, and details that reflect your situation.

Epilogue

As I come to the end of this book, my overriding sentiment is amazement. I am amazed that I am done. I am amazed at how profoundly difficult this task was at times. And I am amazed at the grace that has brought me through. I chose to focus my graduate studies and primary vocation in the field of Christian education because I believe that hope for the church and for its witness to the world lies in our ability to live and nurture authentic discipleship. The content of this book is, therefore, dear to my heart, and I have dreamed of putting it into print for many years. When I imagine a life's dream being fulfilled, I usually picture it in isolation, forgetting that everything we do is accomplished in the context of day-to-day life. For me that context has included the demands of a pretty intense job, the struggles of living with a chronic illness, and sad news from dear friends and family about loss of health, homes, employment, and loved ones. My context has also included celebrating the sixteenth birthday of my profoundly intelligent and gentle-spirited nephew, Tristan (what was I busy doing while he was growing up so quickly?), enjoying unexpected and surprisingly pleasurable visits to and from friends (I am the poster child for introversion), and sitting on our tiny concrete slab "patio" listening to house finches and watching my husband feed peanuts to blue jays while contemplating his return to pastoral ministry. No doubt my real-life context has had an unanticipated impact on this work. That I was waiting so long and gathering ideas all along the way meant that I was tempted at times to say everything I've ever thought of on a given topic. At one point when

I felt particularly blocked, my husband advised me to pay attention not to what I wanted to say but to what needed to be said. No doubt I have said many things that I wanted to say and a few things that might better have been left unsaid. My hope is that in some approximation I have also said some things that needed to be said.

As I wrote, I always thought about those who would read this book. I wondered how my personal stories would be heard and about the places where I might have been stepping on sacred territory. I speculated that I might be labeled as liberal by some and conservative by others, as too foundational or as too emergent, or as cynical or even as naïvely idealistic. I fretted a bit about the imagined disappointment of some readers who want more concrete "how-tos" and step-by-step guidance for turning others into Christian disciples. I supposed they might declare this book to be not about Christian education but about theology or ecclesiology. I responded in my imagination that educational ministry is a living process, not readily itemized, and ultimately about "ologies" because our beliefs drive our practice. As I wrote, I was also compelled to be a learner, as I've suggested all disciples are throughout their lives. Some long-held ideas were challenged, some new ideas welcomed, and some latent ideas reclaimed. I rediscovered many dear old friends. Thinkers like William Stringfellow, Parker Palmer, and Marianne Sawicki spoke to me anew; and former passions and commitments came back with renewed life—all of which helped me to face down some resurfacing demons in new ways. It will take some time for me to appreciate the impact of this time of revisiting ideas, doing research, and trying to formulate meaningful constructs out of nascent thoughts. I look forward to that process, and I am eager to welcome your input into that process with me. At best, the written word presents ideas whose practical import can be tested in the real world. I would love to hear from you about how the thoughts in this book strike you and how you see them working or not working in your contexts. I have, therefore, set up a dedicated e-mail address for readers of this book: *cwilliamed@aol.com*. It is my hope that here and there, now and then, you might have encountered the language of grace spoken from these pages and that in the days to come we might participate together in graceful conversations about being and nurturing followers of Jesus in the community of faith.

Notes

Introduction

1. From a homily given by Archbishop Oscar Romero on Good
   Friday, April 13, 1979; James R. Brockman, S. J., ed. and
   trans., *The Church Is All of You: Thoughts of Archbishop Oscar
   Romero* (Minneapolis: Winston Press, 1984), 75.
2. A recent Barna research update reports the declining reputation of Christianity, especially among sixteen- to twenty-
   nine-year-olds, as one of the most important shifts in the
   United States today. "Barna Update: A New Generation
   Expresses its Skepticism and Frustration with Christianity,"
   www.barna.org, accessed July 24, 2008.
3. I am indebted to Sara P. Little, Ph.D., professor emeritus of
   Christian education at Union Seminary/Presbyterian School
   of Christian Education, for her insight and for her enthusi-
   astic support of the initial research that forms the basis of
   this book. Her remarkable career includes serving as the first
   woman professor at Union Seminary in Virginia, developing
   the Ed.D. program at Presbyterian School of Christian Education, holding a professorship at Pacific School of Religion,
   and being the first female recipient of the Distinguished
   Service Award from the Association of Theological Schools

(1994) and of the 2002 Award for Excellence in Theological
Education from the Committee on Theological Education of
the Presbyterian Church (U.S.A.).

4. "Orientation," Leadership Tape 1, side 1, session 2 (Waco,
Tex.: Word, Inc., 1977). William Stringfellow notes the resistance of the church to Nazi totalitarianism as an example of
the "here and there, now and then" expression of the church's
authentic vocation (*An Ethic for Christians and Other Aliens
in a Strange Land* [Waco, Tex.: Word, 1973], 122). In the leadership tapes, Stringfellow questions the church's preoccupation with models and spatial ways of thinking in which the
church is considered a place rather than a moment, an event
that happens in the middle of time, in history, and that transcends time itself. A lawyer by profession and a renowned
lay theologian, Stringfellow died in 1980. He committed
himself to activism against the "principalities and powers"
of systemic evil and worked chiefly in Harlem representing
African Americans who were largely excluded from public
services in the 1960s and 1970s. Stringfellow was a prolific
writer, and his thought, which sounds eerily pertinent to our
current age, is profoundly relevant for the life of the church
in its present-day circumstance. Other titles include *Con-
science and Obedience* (Waco, Tex.: Word, 1977); *A Simplicity
of Faith: My Experience in Mourning* (Nashville: Abingdon,
1982); and *The Politics of Spirituality* (Philadelphia: Westminster, 1984).

Chapter 1

1. Luke Timothy Johnson, *The Writings of the New Testament:
An Interpretation* (Philadelphia: Fortress, 1986), 45.

2. For more on the subject of the socio-political context of
Jesus's ministry, see Luke Timothy Johnson, *The Writings of
the New Testament*; Howard Clark McKee, *Christian Origins
in Sociological Perspective* (Philadelphia: Westminster, 1980);
Bruce J. Malina, *The New Testament World: Insights from Cul-

tural Anthropology (Louisville, Ky.: Westminster John Knox, 1993); or James G. Crossley, *Why Christianity Happened: A Sociohistorical Account of Christian Origins (25–50 CE)* (Louisville, Ky.: Westminster John Knox, 2006). For a compelling discussion of the limitations of sociological models for the study of first-century Palestine and an intriguing alternative approach, see Marianne Sawicki, *Crossing Galilee: Architectures of Contact in the Occupied Land of Jesus* (Harrisburg, Pa.: Trinity International Press, 2000).

3. John Dominic Crossan, *The Birth of Christianity: Discovering What Happened in the Years Immediately after the Execution of Jesus* (New York: HarperCollins, 1998), ix; and Christoph Burchard, "Jesus of Nazareth" in Jurgen Becker, ed., *Christian Beginnings: Word and Community from Jesus to Post-apostolic Times* (Louisville, Ky.: Westminster John Knox, 1993), 21.

4. William Stringfellow, *An Ethic for Christians and Other Aliens in a Strange Land* (Eugene, Ore.: Wipf & Stock Publishers), 19.

Chapter 2

1. Crossan, *The Birth of Christianity*, ix–x. Crossan provides a fascinating, if somewhat controversial, reconstruction of Christianity in the first two decades after Jesus's death and resurrection.

2. James D. G. Dunn, *Unity and Diversity in the New Testament: An Inquiry into the Character of Earlist Christianity,* 2nd ed. (Philadelphia: Trinity Press International, 1990), identifies the following texts as examples of the earliest Palestinian hymns: Luke 1:46–55, 1:68–79, 2:14, 2:29–32 (p. 132). He provides extensive research on the early communities, their beliefs, practices, and distinctives. I am also indebted to this work for the identification of the primary confessions mentioned in this chapter.

3. There has been an explosion of interest in the role of James, the brother of Jesus, in the past decade, partly inspired by the discovery of an ossuary that was thought to contain his remains. Those who want to learn more about James and the

Jerusalem church should consult John Painter, *Just James: The Brother of Jesus in History and Tradition* (Minneapolis: Fortress, 1999), or the essays on James in Bruce Chilton and Jacob Neusner, eds., *The Brother of Jesus: James the Just and His Mission* (Louisville, Ky.: Westminster John Knox, 2002).

4. For more on the collection of oral traditions, see Richard A. Edwards, *A Theology of Q* (Philadelphia: Fortress, 1976); "Jesus in the Memory of the Church" in Luke Timothy Johnson, *The Writings of the New Testament*; and James D. G. Dunn, "Primitive Confessional Formula," *Unity and Diversity in the New Testament: An Inquiry into the Character of Earliest Christianity*, 2nd ed. (Philadelphia: Trinity Press International, 1990).

5. For more on teaching in the apostolic age and on the role of traveling Christian prophets and their oversight of baptism as a rite of initiation, see Reginald Fuller's "Christian Initiation in the New Testament" in *Made Not Born: New Perspectives on Christian Initiation and the Catechumenate* by Murphy Center for Liturgical Research (South Bend, Ind.: University of Notre Dame Press, 1976). The Didache, a two-part tract containing a moral code for Christians and a manual of church order, also offers guidelines for welcoming traveling Christian prophets (12:1–13:3) and includes details for preparing converts for baptism and participation in Christian community. Scholars disagree about when this work was written, dating it as early as 40 CE and as late as the mid-second century. One good study and translation (it was written in Greek) is Aaron Milavec, *The Didache: Text, Translation, Analysis, and Commentary* (Collegeville, Minn.: Liturgical Press, 2003); Milavec argues for a very early date. I've opted not to use the Didache as a primary source because of the difficulty in dating the document and because of overreliance on the source in histories of Christian education as evidence of catechesis in the first century. See also chapter 4 of *The Gospel in History: Portrait of a Teaching Church, The Origins of Christian Education* (New York: Paulist Press, 1988), in which phenomenologist Marianne

Sawicki (one who studies the structures of experience and the meanings things have in our experience) offers a profound exploration of the communication of the gospel in the apostolic age.

6. In recent years, some scholars have challenged the traditional notion that Judaism was uniquely monotheistic and even attribute the spread of Christianity (and Islam) in part to an openness among polytheistic religions to the possibility that there was "one God who is the source of it all." A major proponent of this view is James G. Crossley (*Why Christianity Happened*, 98), who relies on research presented in Polymnia Athanassiadi and Michael Freded, ed., *Pagan Monotheism in Late Antiquity* (Oxford, U.K.: Oxford University Press, 1999).

7. Sociological studies help us understand how Christianity made its way from the ministry of a Judean itinerant to the primarily Gentile cities of the Roman Empire. Two such studies that have been helpful in the development of this chapter are Wayne Meeks, *The First Urban Christians: The Social World of the Apostle Paul* (New Haven, Conn.: Yale University Press, 1983), and James G. Crossley, *Why Christianity Happened* (Louisville: Westminster John Knox, 2006).

Chapter 3

1. Robert Browning, "A Death in the Desert," lines 126–33, from *Dramatic's Personae* (London: Chapman and Hall, 1864), 91.

2. In his book *The Churches the Apostles Left Behind* (Mahwah, N.J.: Paulist Press, 1984), Raymond Brown defines the apostolic age as the second third of the first century. The last third of the first century he dubs the Sub-Apostolic Period, because it was a period when authority lay in apostolic adherence, as evidenced in the practice of writing letters in the names of the apostles. This commitment to apostolic adherence contrasts with the post-apostolic period of the next century, when Christian leaders, such as the church fathers, wrote on their own authority (pp. 15–16). Brown's work,

along with that of Dunn (*Unity and Diversity in the New Testament*), has been helpful in identifying key communities as they are reflected in the writings of the New Testament.

3. I am following the lead of Brown, Dunn, and the majority of New Testament scholars in assigning authorship of the letters of Colossians, Ephesians, and 1 and 2 Timothy and Titus to the Pauline school after Paul's death. It is beyond the scope of this work to debate authorship. My choice to follow majority scholarship on the dating and authorship is a functional one, as it allows us to group for discussion those letters that reflect communities that responded in similar ways to the question of how to continue into the next generation. For example, Colossians and Ephesians both suggest communities with a focus on the idealized church, and the Pastorals all reflect communities with structure developed well beyond the charismatic model of Paul's time. It was common practice in the first century to write in the name of one's teacher, both to honor him and to claim apostolic authority for the writing. This claim to authority is one of the distinctive characteristics, as mentioned above, of what Brown calls the *Sub*-Apostolic period as opposed to the *post*-apostolic, which proceeds on independent authority. Having reviewed the scholarship, Brown accesses the opinion on deutero-Pauline authorship of disputed letters as follows:

> By way of very broad approximation, about 90 percent of critical scholarship judges that Paul did not write the Pastorals, 80 percent that he did not write Ephesians, and 60 percent that he did not write Colossians (*The Churches the Apostles Left Behind*, 47).

4. For more on the development of the Community of the Beloved Disciple, see Raymond Brown, *The Community of the Beloved Disciple: The Life, Loves, and Hates of an Individual Church in New Testament Times* (New York: Paulist Press, 1979); and Stephen L. Harris, *Introduction to the New Testa-*

ment (Mountain View, Calif.: Mayfield Publishing Company, 1995), 164–67.

Chapter 4

1. Parker Palmer, *To Know as We Are Known: Education as Spiritual Journey* (New York: HarperCollins, 1993), 113.
2. *Webster's II New Riverside University Dictionary* (New York: Riverside Publishing, 1988) s.v. "teach."
3. Ibid., s.v. "educate."
4. Johnson, *The Writings of the New Testament*, 458. Martin Luther did not include the book of James among what he terms the "chief and proper books," because he thought it contradicted Paul's teaching on faith righteousness and did not "show thee Christ." This view, according to Johnson, was adopted "with a vengeance" by nineteenth-century critiques (p. 453).
5. Palmer, *To Know as We Are Known*, 107–8.
6. "Living in Hope" in *An Ethic for Christians and Other Aliens in a Strange Land*, Programmed Leadership Tapes (Waco, Tex.: Word, Inc., 1977), cassette 3, session 10.
7. Palmer, *To Know as We Are Known*, 113.
8. Geoffrey Wigoder, gen. ed., *Illustrated Dictionary and Concordance of the Bible* (Jerusalem: G. G. The Jerusalem Publishing House, Ltd., 1986), 283.

Chapter 5

1. Dunn, *Unity and Diversity in the New Testament: An Inquiry into the Character of Earliest Christianity* 2nd ed. (Philadelphia: Trinity Press International, 1990), 376.
2. Ibid., 59.
3. For more on this pivotal biblical concept, see John Bright's classic *The Kingdom of God* (New York: Abingdon, 1953).

4. Texts that speak to the presence of Jesus through the Spirit include: (in the gathered community) Matthew 18:20, Acts 2:1–12; 1 John 3:19–24; Romans 4:9–13; Galatians 5:22–23; 1 Corinthians 12:27, Ephesians 1:21, Colossians 1:8; (as master teacher and guide) John 14:15–17, 25–26; John 16:26; 16:4–15; Acts 4:8, 31; (indwelling and gifting believers) Acts 1:8; 2:14–25; Romans 8:1–17, 1 Corinthians 5:4; 12; 13; 14; (to the world through proclamation) Acts 4:8, 31; 6:3–5; 8:29; 13:2–9; John 15:18–26.

5. Marianne Sawicki, *The Gospel in History*, 28.

6. "Christ's Body" from *Eerdmans' Book of Famous Prayers* (Grand Rapids, Mich.: Eerdmans, 1984), 51.

7. *Theological Dictionary of the New Testament*, vol. 2, *elachiston*, 697–98.

8. For more on dominion, see Andrew Linzey, *Animal Gospel* (Louisville, Ky.: Westminster John Knox, 1998), especially chapters 4 and 16; and Andrew Linzey, *Animal Theology* (Chicago: University of Illinois Press, 1995), especially chapter 3.

9. Samuel Taylor Coleridge, "The Rime of the Ancient Mariner," *Lyrical Ballads with a Few Other Poems* by William Wordsworth and Samuel Taylor Coleridge (London: T.N. Longman, 1798), 1–52.

10. Samuel Butler, *Hudibras: In Three Parts, Written in the Time of the Late Wars*, part ii, canto I, line 843 (Cambridge: J. Bentham, 1774), 349.

11. References to Mary Magdalene include Matthew 27:55–56; 28:1–8; Mark 16:1–8; 40–41; Luke 8:1–3; 23:55; 24:1–12; John 20:1–10, 17.

12. "James Herriot: Portrait of a Bestseller," presented by Melvyn Bragg; Bob Lockyer, producer, 1976. From *All Creatures Great and Small: The Complete Series 1 Collection* (BBC Worldwide Americas, Inc., 1978).

Chapter 6

1. Wayne Meeks, *The First Urban Christians*, 145–46.
2. Sara Little, *To Set One's Heart*, 87–88.
3. Bruce Malina and Jerome H. Neyrey, "The Problem of Ancient Personality" in *Portraits of Paul: An Archaeology of Ancient Personality* (Louisville, Ky.: Westminster John Knox, 1996) 16–17. While the writers' interest lies in a particular segment of the population of early Christians, namely the Pauline communities, it can be readily argued that the collectivist mentality that is present among them is also clearly evident within the Palestinian context. Appendix 2 of *Portraits of Paul* provides a chart that contrasts contemporary Western and ancient Mediterranean culture. It is worth a look for anyone interested in a better understanding of life in New Testament times.
4. *Webster's II New Riverside University Dictionary* s.v. "radical."
5. Mariane Sawicki, *The Gospel in History*, 39.
6. See *metecho* and *koinonos* in *Theological Dictionary of the New Testament*, vol. 2, 830, and vol. 3, 796 ff.
7. Dunn, *Unity and Diversity in the New Testament*, 57.
8. The departure of the root group of the Johannine community from the Palestinian church, which was precipitated by their emphasis on Jesus's divinity, might also fit into the category of a break over doctrine. I have not mentioned it here, because while the event is suggested by Raymond Brown's scholarly and well-supported reconstruction, it is not directly attested to in the New Testament.
9. Sara Little, *To Set One's Heart*, 28.
10. *The Lion Encyclopedia of the Bible* (Batavia, Ill.: Lion Publishing, 1986), 135, 138–39.
11. Mark 9:15–37,10:13–16; Matthew 17:14–18,18:1–6, 19:13–15, 21:14–16; Luke 9:46–48, 17:1–3, 18:15–17; and John 6:1–15.
12. Judy Gundry-Volf, "The Least and the Greatest: Children in the New Testament" in Marcia J. Bunge, ed., *The Child in Christian Thought* (Grand Rapids, Mich.: Eerdmans, 2001), 60.

13. This phenomenon was challenged by nineteenth-century Congregational pastor Horace Bushnell in a series of discourses in the Massachusetts Sunday School Society that were later published as the Christian education classic *Christian Nurture*. Bushnell challenged the prevailing notion—an inheritance of American Revivalism—that true conversion hinged on a single emotional experience. He believed that this requirement left children spiritually disenfranchised, guilty of sin but lacking the maturity to undergo the adult experience of conversion. One of the earliest and strongest proponents of Christian education as socialization, Bushnell advanced an understanding of conversion as a natural process in which all children will become Christian if they are treated as full participants in the community. While over-optimistic, it continues to serve as a corrective to those who "school" children in Christian faith, while leaving them on the margins of church life. First published in 1847, *Christian Nurture* is still produced by Baker Book House, Grand Rapids, Michigan.

14. Thank you to Paul Walaskay, professor of biblical studies at Union/PSCE, for taking my phone call and confirming for me the importance of Luke's stipulation that Peter reached out his right hand. This understanding of the healing of the lame man as more than physical healing is confirmed by William H. Willimon in *Acts* from the series *Interpretation: A Bible Commentary for Teaching and Preaching* (Atlanta: John Knox, 1988), 44–45.

15. Christianity was declared the official religion of the Roman Empire under Constantine (285–337 CE), who presided over a conference at Nicaea in which he mandated that church leaders determine official Christian doctrine. Called on to legitimate the empire, the church abandoned much of its social critique and in return received status and power.

16. Stringfellow, *An Ethic for Christian and Other Aliens in a Strange Land*, 138. The comments in this section are drawn from his profound treatment of the spiritual gifts (pp. 137–56).

17. Ibid., 140.

18. Ibid., 140–41.

19. David White, *Practicing Discernment with Youth: A Transformative Youth Ministry Approach* (Cleveland: Pilgrim Press, 2005), 65. This remarkable treatment is not only a must-read for anyone who presumes to guide youth in the way of discipleship, but also an excellent resource for adults who wish to move from "faith to greater faith" (p. 84).

20. Ibid., 88.

21. *Postmodern Children's Ministry: Ministry to Children in the 21st Century* (Grand Rapids, Mich.: Zondervan, 2004), 101–2.

22. Samuel Butler, *Hudibras,* part ii, canto I, lines 840–43, 349.

23. Judith M. Gundry-Volf, "The Least and the Greatest," 53–60. In her analysis of the household codes found in Colossians and Ephesians, Gundry-Volf concludes: "The household codes reflect some of the emphases of Jesus's teaching on children, but not the most radical valorizations of children. In Colossians and Ephesians, children are viewed as members of the community of believers but not as models for adult believers or as spiritually insightful. These roles that children have in Jesus's teaching have been eclipsed by the roles of others in the early church and by children's own roles in the family." This phenomenon is in keeping with the concern of the later Pauline churches to demonstrate that they are not a threat within the empire.

24. Sources: Elizabeth Gershoff, "Corporal Punishment by Parents and Associated Child Behaviors and Experiences: A Meta-Analytic and Theoretical Review," *Psychological Bulletin* 128, no. 4 (July 2002): 539–79, *www.apa.org/,* can also be found at *www.endcorporalpunishment.org/pages/pdfs/Gershoff-2002.pdf;* Adah Maurer, Ph.D., and James S. Wallerstein, "The Influence of Corporal Punishment on Crime" (1987), online at the The Natural Child Project, *www.naturalchild.org/research/corporal_punishment.html;* Andrew Grogan-Kaylor, "The Effect of Corporal Punishment on Antisocial Behavior in Children," *Social Work Research* 28, no. 3 (Sept. 2004): 153–62, abstract available at *sitemaker.umich.edu/grogan-kaylor/research_on_corporal_punishment;* American

Psychological Association, "Is Corporal Punishment an Effective Means of Discipline?" APA online media information
press release, June 26, 2002, *www.apa.org/releases/spanking.
html*; Alice Miller, Ph.D., "Reflections on Spanking," online at
The Natural Child Project, *www.naturalchild.org/alice_miller/
spanking.html*; "Spanking Kids Increases Risk of Sexual
Problems as Adults, New Research Shows," The Natural
Child Project, Feb. 28, 2008, *www.naturalchild.org/research/
spanking_problems.html*, which cites the research of Murray
Strauss, Ph.D., professor of sociology and codirector, Family
Research Laboratory, University of New Hampshire, Durham, New Hampshire. More on Dr. Strauss can be found on
his home page, *pubpages.unh.edu/~mas2/* and his empirical
studies on corporal punishment, *pubpages.unh.edu/~mas2/
CP-Empirical.htm*; Murray A. Straus, Ph.D., David B. Sugar-
man, Ph.D., Jean Giles-Sims, Ph.D., "Spanking by Parents
and Subsequent Antisocial Behavior of Children," *Archives of
Pediatric and Adolescent Medicine* 1997, 151:761–67, available
at *www.geocities.com/kidhistory/ja/spankms.htm* or through
the Family Research Laboratory, University of New Hampshire, Durham, New Hampshire, *www.unh.edu/frl/cbb.htm*.

Chapter 7

1. Little, *To Set One's Heart*, 87.
2. Dunn, *Unity and Diversity in the New Testament*, 77.
3. In his groundbreaking work *The Eclipse of Biblical Narrative*
    (New Haven, Conn.: Yale University Press, 1974), Hans Frei
    offered, in the midst of what I consider a somewhat skewed
    treatment of historical-critical method, a much-needed re-
    minder of the narrative integrity of the New Testament. His
    thought provided a "lightbulb" experience for me in which
    I came to view all of Scripture, from the obviously narrative
    Gospels to the less obvious legal material and Proverbs, as nar-
    rative. For a useful summary of the ways the message of Scrip-

ture has been appropriated, see David Kelsey, *Uses of Scripture in Recent Theology* (Philadelphia: Fortress, 1975).

4. Sources: *The Learning Bible*, 11–13; "Bible Translations" in *Illustrated Dictionary of the Bible*, 181–84.

5. Sawicki, *The Gospel in History*, 8.

6. Dunn, *Unity and Diversity in the New Testament*, 57.

7. Ibid.

8. Instances include Acts 2:36; 5:42; 9:20, 22; 10:36; 11:20; 17:3; 18:5, 28; John 9:22; 12:42; 20:28; Romans 1:3; 10:9; 1 Corinthians 1:23; 12:3; 16:22; 2 Corinthians 4:5; Philippians 2:11; Colossians 2:6; 1 John 2:18–23; 4:1–3.

9. The bishop in question was Alexander of Alexandria. The quote is taken from Kenneth Scott Latourette, *A History of Christianity* (New York: Harper & Brothers, 1953), 153, and this summary is based on Latourette's treatment on pp. 152–55.

10. Renita J. Weems, "Reading *Her Way* through the Struggle: African American Women and the Bible," in Cain Hope Felder, ed., *Stony the Way We Trod: African American Biblical Interpretation* (Minneapolis: Fortress, 1991), 67.

11. The Scofield Reference Bible, first published in 1909 by Oxford University Press.

12. "The Power of the Storyteller in Religious Education," *Religious Education* 102, no. 3 (summer 2007), 296.

13. Sources: Latourette, *A History of Christianity,* 799, 805, 817; Gail R. O'Day and David Peterson, eds., Preface to *The Access Bible: An Ecumenical Learning Resource for People of Faith* (New York and Oxford: Oxford University Press, 1991), vii–viii; Stephen L. Harris, *Introduction to the New Testament,* 20.

14. "Perfect Prophets, Helpful Hippos, and Happy Endings: Noah and Jonah in Children's Bible Storybooks in the United States," in *Religious Education* 102, no. 3 (summer 2007): 298; Carolyn Baker Nabors, *The Beginners Bible Tales of Virtue: A Book of Right and Wrong* (New York: Little Moorings Press, 1995), 81, as quoted in "Perfect Prophets, Helpful Hippos, and Happy Endings," 302.

15. While Dalton does not provide statistical data in his article, he cites more than thirty titles, with publication dates beginning as early as 1750, that evidence these practices.
16. Russ Dalton, "Perfect Prophets, Helpful Hippos, and Happy Endings," 299.
17. I reviewed several mission statements from churches in the area and found statements similar to this one present in all of them.
18. Dunn, *Unity and Diversity in the New Testament,* 54. Dunn argues, convincingly in my opinion, against the traditional view that the association of creeds with baptism and the Lord's Supper was present in New Testament times.
19. White, *Practicing Discernment with Youth,* 65.
20. Dunn, *Unity and Diversity in the New Testament,* 57.
21. Little, *To Set One's Heart,* 90.
22. *Dei Verbum* No. 8, "The Dogmatic Constitution on Divine Revelation" of the Second Vatican Council, as quoted by Marianne Sawicki, *The Gospel in History,* 8.

Conclusion

1. Dietrich Bonhoeffer, *The Cost of Discipleship;* R. H. Fuller, trans. (London: SCM Press, 1956), 162.